Contents

QUICK AND EASY CHICKEN NOODLE SOUP

Servings: 6 - Prep: 10m - Cooks: 20m - Total: 30m

NUTRITION FACTS

Calories: 161, Carbohydrates: 12.1g, Fat: 6.1g, Protein: 13.4g, Cholesterol: 46mg

INGREDIENTS

- 1 tablespoon butter
- 1 1/2 cups egg noodles
- 1/2 cup chopped onion
- 1 cup sliced carrots
- 1/2 cup chopped celery
- 1/2 teaspoon dried basil
- 4 (14.5 ounce) cans chicken broth
- 1/2 teaspoon dried oregano
- 1 (14.5 ounce) can vegetable broth
- salt and pepper to taste
- 1/2 pound chopped cooked chicken breast

DIRECTIONS

1. In a large pot over medium heat, melt butter. Cook onion and celery in butter until just tender, 5 minutes. Pour in chicken and vegetable broths and stir in chicken, noodles, carrots, basil, oregano, salt and pepper. Bring to a boil, then reduce heat and simmer 20 minutes before serving.

CREAMY CAJUN CHICKEN PASTA

Servings: 2 - Prep: 15m - Cooks: 15m - Total: 30m

NUTRITION FACTS

Calories: 1109, Carbohydrates: 53.7g, Fat: 82.2g, Protein: 42.7g, Cholesterol: 348mg

INGREDIENTS

- 4 ounces linguine pasta
- 1 1/2 cups heavy cream
- 2 boneless, skinless chicken breast halves, sliced into thin strips
- 1/4 teaspoon dried basil

- 2 teaspoons Cajun seasoning
- 1/4 teaspoon lemon pepper
- 2 tablespoons butter
- 1/4 teaspoon salt
- 1 green bell pepper, chopped
- 1/8 teaspoon garlic powder
- 1/2 red bell pepper, chopped
- 1/8 teaspoon ground black pepper
- 4 fresh mushrooms, sliced
- 2 tablespoons grated Parmesan cheese
- 1 green onion, minced

DIRECTIONS

1. Bring a large pot of lightly salted water to a boil. Add linguini pasta, and cook for 8 to 10 minutes, or until al dente; drain.
2. Meanwhile, place chicken and Cajun seasoning in a bowl, and toss to coat.
3. In a large skillet over medium heat, saute chicken in butter until no longer pink and juices run clear, about 5 to 7 minutes. Add green and red bell peppers, sliced mushrooms and green onions; cook for 2 to 3 minutes. Reduce heat, and stir in heavy cream. Season the sauce with basil, lemon pepper, salt, garlic powder and ground black pepper, and heat through.
4. In a large bowl, toss linguini with sauce. Sprinkle with grated Parmesan cheese.

CHICKEN MILANO

Servings: 4 - Prep: 10m - Cooks: 20m - Total: 30m

NUTRITION FACTS

Calories: 641, Carbohydrates: 47g, Fat: 34.8g, Protein: 36.3g, Cholesterol: 156mg

INGREDIENTS

- 1 tablespoon butter
- 1 pound skinless, boneless chicken breast halves
- 2 cloves garlic, minced
- salt and pepper to taste
- 1/2 cup sun-dried tomatoes, chopped
- 2 tablespoons vegetable oil
- 1 cup chicken broth, divided
- 2 tablespoons chopped fresh basil

- 1 cup heavy cream
- 8 ounces dry fettuccini pasta

DIRECTIONS

1. In a large saucepan over low heat, melt butter; add garlic and cook for 30 seconds. Add the tomatoes and 3/4 cup of the chicken broth; increase to medium heat and bring to a boil. Reduce heat and simmer, uncovered, for about 10 minutes or until the tomatoes are tender. Add the cream and bring to a boil; stirring. Simmer over medium heat until the sauce is thick enough to coat the back of a spoon.

2. Sprinkle the chicken with salt and pepper on both sides. In a large skillet over medium heat, warm oil and saute chicken. Press on chicken occasionally with a slotted spatula. Cook for about 4 minutes per side or until the meat feels springy and is no longer pink inside. Transfer to a board; cover and keep warm. Discard the fat from the skillet.

3. In the same skillet, over medium heat, bring 1/4 cup chicken broth to a boil; stirring the pan juices. Reduce slightly and add to the cream sauce; stir in basil and adjust seasonings to taste.

4. Meanwhile, bring a large pot of lightly salted water to a boil. Add fettuccine and cook for 8 to 10 minutes or until al dente; drain, transfer to a bowl and toss with 3 to 4 tablespoons of the sauce.

5. Cut each chicken breast into 2 to 3 diagonal slices. Reheat the sauce gently if needed. Transfer the pasta to serving plates; top with chicken and coat with the cream sauce; serve.

ITALIAN SAUSAGE SOUP WITH TORTELLINI

Servings: 8 - Prep: 20m - Cooks: 1h15m - Total: 1h35m

NUTRITION FACTS

Calories: 324, Carbohydrates: 19.1g, Fat: 20.1g, Protein: 14.6g, Cholesterol: 50mg

INGREDIENTS

- 1 pound sweet Italian sausage, casings removed
- 1 cup thinly sliced carrots
- 1 cup chopped onion
- 1/2 tablespoon packed fresh basil leaves
- 2 cloves garlic, minced
- 1/2 teaspoon dried oregano
- 5 cups beef broth
- 1 (8 ounce) can tomato sauce
- 1/2 cup water

- 1 1/2 cups sliced zucchini
- 1/2 cup red wine
- 8 ounces fresh tortellini pasta
- 4 large tomatoes - peeled, seeded and chopped
- 3 tablespoons chopped fresh parsley

DIRECTIONS

1. In a 5 quart Dutch oven, brown sausage. Remove sausage and drain, reserving 1 tablespoon of the drippings.

2. Saute onions and garlic in drippings. Stir in beef broth, water, wine, tomatoes, carrots, basil, oregano, tomato sauce, and sausage. Bring to a boil. Reduce heat; simmer uncovered for 30 minutes.

3. Skim fat from the soup. Stir in zucchini and parsley. Simmer covered for 30 minutes. Add tortellini during the last 10 minutes. Sprinkle with Parmesan cheese on top of each serving.

AMERICAN LASAGNA

Servings: 8 - Prep: 30m - Cooks: 1h15m - Total: 1h55m - Additional: 10m

NUTRITION FACTS

Calories: 664, Carbohydrates: 48.3g, Fat: 29.5g, Protein: 50.9g, Cholesterol: 168mg

INGREDIENTS

- 1 1/2 pounds lean ground beef
- 2 (6 ounce) cans tomato paste
- 1 onion, chopped
- 12 dry lasagna noodles
- 2 cloves garlic, minced
- 2 eggs, beaten
- 1 tablespoon chopped fresh basil
- 1 pint part-skim ricotta cheese
- 1 teaspoon dried oregano
- 1/2 cup grated Parmesan cheese
- 2 tablespoons brown sugar
- 2 tablespoons dried parsley
- 1 1/2 teaspoons salt
- 1 teaspoon salt
- 1 (29 ounce) can diced tomatoes
- 1 pound mozzarella cheese, shredded

- 1 1/2 pounds lean ground beef
- 2 tablespoons grated Parmesan cheese

DIRECTIONS

1. In a skillet over medium heat, brown ground beef, onion and garlic for 5 minutes; drain fat. Mix in basil, oregano, brown sugar, 1 1/2 teaspoons salt, diced tomatoes and tomato paste. Simmer for 30 to 45 minutes, stirring occasionally.
2. Preheat oven to 375 degrees F (190 degrees C). Bring a large pot of lightly salted water to a boil. Add lasagna noodles, and cook for 5 to 8 minutes, or until al dente; drain. Lay noodles flat on towels, and blot dry.
3. In a medium bowl, mix together eggs, ricotta, Parmesan cheese, parsley and 1 teaspoon salt.
4. Layer 1/3 of the lasagna noodles in the bottom of a 9x13 inch baking dish. Cover noodles with 1/2 ricotta mixture, 1/2 of the mozzarella cheese and 1/3 of the sauce. Repeat. Top with remaining noodles and sauce. Sprinkle additional Parmesan cheese over the top.
5. Bake in the preheated oven 30 minutes. Let stand 10 minutes before serving.

BEST TUNA CASSEROLE

Servings: 6 - Prep: 15m - Cooks: 20m - Total: 35m

NUTRITION FACTS

Calories: 595, Carbohydrates: 58.1g, Fat: 26.1g, Protein: 32.1g, Cholesterol: 99mg

INGREDIENTS

- 1 (12 ounce) package egg noodles
- 2 (5 ounce) cans tuna, drained
- 1/4 cup chopped onion
- 2 (10.75 ounce) cans condensed cream of mushroom soup
- 2 cups shredded Cheddar cheese
- 1/2 (4.5 ounce) can sliced mushrooms
- 1 cup frozen green peas
- 1 cup crushed potato chips

DIRECTIONS

1. Bring a large pot of lightly salted water to a boil. Cook pasta in boiling water for 8 to 10 minutes, or until al dente; drain.
2. Preheat oven to 425 degrees F (220 degrees C).
3. In a large bowl, thoroughly mix noodles, onion, 1 cup cheese, peas, tuna, soup and mushrooms. Transfer to a 9x13 inch baking dish, and top with potato chip crumbs and remaining 1 cup cheese.

4. Bake for 15 to 20 minutes in the preheated oven, or until cheese is bubbly.

CLASSIC MACARONI SALAD

Servings: 10 - Prep: 20m - Cooks: 10m - Total: 4h30m

NUTRITION FACTS

Calories: 390, Carbohydrates: 49.3g, Fat: 18.7g, Protein: 6.8g, Cholesterol: 8mg

INGREDIENTS

- 4 cups uncooked elbow macaroni
- 1/2 teaspoon ground black pepper
- 1 cup mayonnaise
- 1 large onion, chopped
- 1/4 cup distilled white vinegar
- 2 stalks celery, chopped
- 2/3 cup white sugar
- 1 green bell pepper, seeded and chopped
- 2 1/2 tablespoons prepared yellow mustard
- 1/4 cup grated carrot (optional)
- 1 1/2 teaspoons salt
- 2 tablespoons chopped pimento peppers (optional)

DIRECTIONS

1. Bring a large pot of lightly salted water to a boil. Add the macaroni, and cook until tender, about 8 minutes. Rinse under cold water and drain.

2. In a large bowl, mix together the mayonnaise, vinegar, sugar, mustard, salt and pepper. Stir in the onion, celery, green pepper, carrot, pimentos and macaroni. Refrigerate for at least 4 hours before serving, but preferably overnight.

CAJUN CHICKEN PASTA

Servings: 2 - Prep: 20m - Cooks: 20m - Total: 40m

NUTRITION FACTS

Calories: 935, Carbohydrates: 54g, Fat: 61.7g, Protein: 43.7g, Cholesterol: 271mg

INGREDIENTS

- 4 ounces linguine pasta
- 1 cup heavy cream
- 2 skinless, boneless chicken breast halves

- 1/4 teaspoon dried basil
- 2 teaspoons Cajun seasoning
- 1/4 teaspoon lemon pepper
- 2 tablespoons butter
- 1/4 teaspoon salt
- 1 red bell pepper, sliced
- 1/8 teaspoon garlic powder
- 1 green bell pepper, sliced
- 1/8 teaspoon ground black pepper
- 4 fresh mushrooms, sliced
- 1/4 cup grated Parmesan cheese
- 1 green onion, chopped

DIRECTIONS

1. Bring a large pot of lightly salted water to a boil. Add pasta and cook for 8 to 10 minutes or until al dente; drain.
2. Place the chicken and the Cajun seasoning in a plastic bag. Shake to coat. In a large skillet over medium heat, saute the chicken in butter or margarine until almost tender (5 to 7 minutes).
3. Add the red bell pepper, green bell pepper, mushrooms and green onion. Saute and stir for 2 to 3 minutes. Reduce heat.
4. Add the cream, basil, lemon pepper, salt, garlic powder and ground black pepper. Heat through. Add the cooked linguine, toss and heat through. Sprinkle with grated Parmesan cheese and serve.

JAMIE'S MINESTRONE

Servings: 8 - Prep: 35m - Cooks: 50m - Total: 1h25m

NUTRITION FACTS

Calories: 227, Carbohydrates: 30g, Fat: 8.3g, Protein: 8.6g, Cholesterol: 1mg

INGREDIENTS

- 3 tablespoons olive oil
- 1 (15 ounce) can green beans
- 3 cloves garlic, chopped
- 2 cups baby spinach, rinsed
- 2 onions, chopped
- 3 zucchinis, quartered and sliced
- 2 cups chopped celery

- 1 tablespoon chopped fresh oregano
- 5 carrots, sliced
- 2 tablespoons chopped fresh basil
- 2 cups chicken broth
- salt and pepper to taste
- 2 cups water
- 1/2 cup seashell pasta
- 4 cups tomato sauce
- 2 tablespoons grated Parmesan cheese for topping
- 1/2 cup red wine (optional)
- 1 tablespoon olive oil
- 1 cup canned kidney beans, drained

DIRECTIONS

1. In a large stock pot, over medium-low heat, heat olive oil and saute garlic for 2 to 3 minutes. Add onion and saute for 4 to 5 minutes. Add celery and carrots, saute for 1 to 2 minutes.

2. Add chicken broth, water and tomato sauce, bring to boil, stirring frequently. If desired add red wine at this point. Reduce heat to low and add kidney beans, green beans, spinach leaves, zucchini, oregano, basil, salt and pepper. Simmer for 30 to 40 minutes, the longer the better.

3. Fill a medium saucepan with water and bring to a boil. Add macaroni and cook until tender. Drain water and set aside.

4. Once pasta is cooked and soup is heated through place 2 tablespoons cooked pasta into individual serving bowls. Ladle soup on top of pasta and sprinkle Parmesan cheese on top. Spray with olive oil and serve.

WHITE CHEESE CHICKEN LASAGNA

Servings: 12 - Prep: 25m - Cooks: 50m - Total: 1h15m

NUTRITION FACTS

Calories: 369, Carbohydrates: 22.8g, Fat: 20.7g, Protein: 23.7g, Cholesterol: 77mg

INGREDIENTS

- 9 lasagna noodles
- 1 teaspoon dried basil
- 1/2 cup butter
- 1 teaspoon dried oregano
- 1 onion, chopped

- 1/2 teaspoon ground black pepper
- 1 clove garlic, minced
- 2 cups ricotta cheese
- 1/2 cup all-purpose flour
- 2 cups cubed, cooked chicken meat
- 1 teaspoon salt
- 2 (10 ounce) packages frozen chopped spinach, thawed and drained
- 2 cups chicken broth
- 1 tablespoon chopped fresh parsley
- 1 1/2 cups milk
- 1/4 cup grated Parmesan cheese for topping
- 4 cups shredded mozzarella cheese, divided
- 1 cup grated Parmesan cheese, divided

DIRECTIONS

1. Preheat oven to 350 degrees F (175 degrees C). Bring a large pot of lightly salted water to a boil. Cook lasagna noodles in boiling water for 8 to 10 minutes. Drain, and rinse with cold water.

2. Melt the butter in a large saucepan over medium heat. Cook the onion and garlic in the butter until tender, stirring frequently. Stir in the flour and salt, and simmer until bubbly. Mix in the broth and milk, and boil, stirring constantly, for 1 minute. Stir in 2 cups mozzarella cheese and 1/4 cup Parmesan cheese. Season with the basil, oregano, and ground black pepper. Remove from heat, and set aside.

3. Spread 1/3 of the sauce mixture in the bottom of a 9x13 inch baking dish. Layer with 1/3 of the noodles, the ricotta, and the chicken. Arrange 1/3 of the noodles over the chicken, and layer with 1/3 of the sauce mixture, spinach, and the remaining 2 cups mozzarella cheese and 1/2 cup Parmesan cheese. Arrange remaining noodles over cheese, and spread remaining sauce evenly over noodles. Sprinkle with parsley and 1/4 cup Parmesan cheese.

4. Bake 35 to 40 minutes in the preheated oven.

HOMEMADE MAC AND CHEESE

Servings: 4 - Prep: 20m - Cooks: 30m - Total: 50m

NUTRITION FACTS

Calories: 858, Carbohydrates: 66.7g, Fat: 48.7g, Protein: 37.7g, Cholesterol: 142mg

INGREDIENTS

- 8 ounces uncooked elbow macaroni
- 2 1/2 tablespoons all-purpose flour

- 2 cups shredded sharp Cheddar cheese
- 2 tablespoons butter
- 1/2 cup grated Parmesan cheese
- 1/2 cup bread crumbs
- 3 cups milk
- 1 pinch paprika
- 1/4 cup butter

DIRECTIONS

1. Cook macaroni according to the package directions. Drain.

2. In a saucepan, melt butter or margarine over medium heat. Stir in enough flour to make a roux. Add milk to roux slowly, stirring constantly. Stir in cheeses, and cook over low heat until cheese is melted and the sauce is a little thick. Put macaroni in large casserole dish, and pour sauce over macaroni. Stir well.

3. Melt butter or margarine in a skillet over medium heat. Add breadcrumbs and brown. Spread over the macaroni and cheese to cover. Sprinkle with a little paprika.

4. Bake at 350 degrees F (175 degrees C) for 30 minutes. Serve.

SPINACH TOMATO TORTELLINI

Servings: 6 - Prep: 20m - Cooks: 20m - Total: 40m

NUTRITION FACTS

Calories: 400, Carbohydrates: 43.9g, Fat: 19.7g, Protein: 14.8g, Cholesterol: 79mg

INGREDIENTS

- 1 (16 ounce) package cheese tortellini
- 1 teaspoon minced garlic
- 1 (14.5 ounce) can diced tomatoes with garlic and onion
- 2 tablespoons all-purpose flour
- 1 cup chopped fresh spinach
- 3/4 cup milk
- 1/2 teaspoon salt
- 3/4 cup heavy cream
- 1/4 teaspoon pepper
- 1/4 cup grated Parmesan cheese
- 1 1/2 teaspoons dried basil

DIRECTIONS

1. Bring a large pot of water to a boil. Add the tortellini, and cook until tender, about 10 minutes.

2. While you get the tortellini going, combine the tomatoes, spinach, salt, pepper, basil and garlic in a large saucepan over medium heat. Cook and stir until the mixture begins to bubble.

3. In a medium bowl, whisk together the flour, milk and cream. Stir this mixture into the saucepan along with the Parmesan cheese. Heat through, then reduce heat to low, and simmer until thick, about 2 minutes.

4. Drain the tortellini, but do not rinse, then pour them into the saucepan with the sauce. Stir to coat, and serve.

CHICKEN NOODLE CASSEROLE

Servings: 6 - Prep: 30m - Cooks: 30m - Total: 1h

NUTRITION FACTS

Calories: 542, Carbohydrates: 35.5g, Fat: 34.2g, Protein: 23.3g, Cholesterol: 133mg

INGREDIENTS

- 4 skinless, boneless chicken breast halves
- salt to taste
- 6 ounces egg noodles
- ground black pepper to taste
- 1 (10.75 ounce) can condensed cream of mushroom soup
- 1 cup crumbled buttery round crackers
- 1 (10.75 ounce) can condensed cream of chicken soup
- 1/2 cup butter
- 1 cup sour cream

DIRECTIONS

1. Poach chicken in a large pot of simmering water. Cook until no longer pink in center, about 12 minutes. Remove from pot and set aside. Bring chicken cooking water to a boil and cook pasta in it. Drain. Cut chicken into small pieces, and mix with noodles.

2. In a separate bowl, mix together mushroom soup, chicken soup, and sour cream. Season with salt and pepper. Gently stir together cream soup mixture with the chicken mixture. Place in a 2 quart baking dish.

3. Melt butter in a small saucepan, and remove from heat. Stir in crumbled crackers. Top casserole with the buttery crackers.

4. Bake at 350 degrees F (175 degrees C) for about 30 minutes, until heated through and browned on top.

PIZZA CASSEROLE

Servings: 7 - Prep: 30m - Cooks: 30m - Total: 1h

NUTRITION FACTS

Calories: 386, Carbohydrates: 17.7g, Fat: 25.3g, Protein: 20.2g, Cholesterol: 79mg

INGREDIENTS

- 2 cups uncooked egg noodles
- 1 cup sliced pepperoni sausage
- 1/2 pound lean ground beef
- 16 ounces pizza sauce
- 1 onion, chopped
- 4 tablespoons milk
- 2 cloves garlic, minced
- 1 cup shredded mozzarella cheese
- 1 green bell pepper, chopped

DIRECTIONS

1. Cook noodles according to package directions.
2. Preheat oven to 350 degrees F (175 degrees C).
3. In a medium skillet over medium-high heat, brown the ground beef with the onion, garlic and green bell pepper. Drain excess fat. Stir in the noodles, pepperoni, pizza sauce and milk, and mix well. Pour this mixture into a 2-quart casserole dish.
4. Bake at 350 degrees F (175 degrees C) for 20 minutes, top with the cheese, then bake for 5 to 10 more minutes.

PEPPERED SHRIMP ALFREDO

Servings: 6 - Prep: 30m - Cooks: 20m - Total: 50m

NUTRITION FACTS

Calories: 707, Carbohydrates: 50.6g, Fat: 45g, Protein: 28.4g, Cholesterol: 201mg

INGREDIENTS

- 12 ounces penne pasta
- 1 pound medium shrimp, peeled and deveined
- 1/4 cup butter
- 1 (15 ounce) jar Alfredo sauce
- 2 tablespoons extra-virgin olive oil

- 1/2 cup grated Romano cheese

- 1 onion, diced

- 1/2 cup cream

- 2 cloves garlic, minced

- 1 teaspoon cayenne pepper, or more to taste

- 1 red bell pepper, diced

- Salt and pepper to taste

- 1/2 pound portobello mushrooms, diced

- 1/4 cup chopped parsley

DIRECTIONS

1. Bring a large pot of lightly salted water to a boil. Add pasta and cook for 8 to 10 minutes or until al dente; drain.

2. Meanwhile, melt butter together with the olive oil in a saucepan over medium heat. Stir in onion, and cook until softened and translucent, about 2 minutes. Stir in garlic, red pepper, and mushroom; cook over medium-high heat until soft, about 2 minutes more.

3. Stir in the shrimp, and cook until firm and pink, then pour in Alfredo sauce, Romano cheese, and cream; bring to a simmer stirring constantly until thickened, about 5 minutes. Season with cayenne, salt, and pepper to taste. Stir drained pasta into the sauce, and serve sprinkled with chopped parsley.

ORZO WITH PARMESAN AND BASIL

Servings: 4 - Prep: 10m - Cooks: 20m - Total: 30m

NUTRITION FACTS

Calories: 299, Carbohydrates: 42.2g, Fat: 9.4g, Protein: 11.6g, Cholesterol: 24mg

INGREDIENTS

- 2 tablespoons butter

- ¼ cup chopped fresh basil

- 1 cup uncooked orzo pasta

- salt and pepper to taste

- 1 (14.5 ounce) can chicken broth

- 2 tablespoons chopped fresh basil

- ½ cup grated Parmesan cheese

DIRECTIONS

1. Melt butter in heavy skillet over medium-high heat. Stir in orzo and saute until lightly browned.

2. Stir in chicken stock and bring to boil. Cover. Reduce heat and simmer until orzo is tender and liquid is absorbed, about 15 - 20 minutes.

3. Mix in Parmesan cheese and basil. Season with salt and pepper. Transfer to shallow bowl. Garnish with basil sprigs.

TO DIE FOR FETTUCCINE ALFREDO

Servings: 6 - Prep: 15m - Cooks: 15m - Total: 30m

NUTRITION FACTS

Calories: 964, Carbohydrates: 84g, Fat: 61.2g, Protein: 23.7g, Cholesterol: 184mg

INGREDIENTS

- 24 ounces dry fettuccini pasta
- 1 dash garlic salt
- 1 cup butter
- 3/4 cup grated Romano cheese
- 3/4 pint heavy cream
- 1/2 cup grated Parmesan cheese
- salt and pepper to taste

DIRECTIONS

1. Bring a large pot of lightly salted water to a boil. Add fettuccini and cook for 8 to 10 minutes or until al dente; drain.

2. In a large saucepan, melt butter into cream over low heat. Add salt, pepper and garlic salt. Stir in cheese over medium heat until melted; this will thicken the sauce.

3. Add pasta to sauce. Use enough of the pasta so that all of the sauce is used and the pasta is thoroughly coated. Serve immediately.

ARTICHOKE SPINACH LASAGNA

Servings: 8 - Prep: 20m - Cooks: 1h - Total: 1h20m

NUTRITION FACTS

Calories: 396, Carbohydrates: 44.5g, Fat: 16g, Protein: 21.1g, Cholesterol: 42mg

INGREDIENTS

- cooking spray
- 1 (14 ounce) can marinated artichoke hearts, drained and chopped
- 9 uncooked lasagna noodles
- 1 (10 ounce) package frozen chopped spinach, thawed, drained and squeezed dry

- 1 onion, chopped
- 1 (28 ounce) jar tomato pasta sauce
- 4 cloves garlic, chopped
- 3 cups shredded mozzarella cheese, divided
- 1 (14.5 ounce) can vegetable broth
- 1 (4 ounce) package herb and garlic feta, crumbled
- 1 tablespoon chopped fresh rosemary

DIRECTIONS

1. Preheat oven to 350 degrees F (175 degrees C). Spray a 9x13 inch baking dish with cooking spray.
2. Bring a large pot of lightly salted water to a boil. Add noodles and cook for 8 to 10 minutes or until al dente; drain.
3. Spray a large skillet with cooking spray and heat on medium-high. Saute onion and garlic for 3 minutes, or until onion is tender-crisp. Stir in broth and rosemary; bring to a boil. Stir in artichoke hearts and spinach; reduce heat, cover and simmer 5 minutes. Stir in pasta sauce.
4. Spread 1/4 of the artichoke mixture in the bottom of the prepared baking dish; top with 3 cooked noodles. Sprinkle 3/4 cup mozzarella cheese over noodles. Repeat layers 2 more times, ending with artichoke mixture and mozzarella cheese. Sprinkle crumbled feta on top.
5. Bake, covered, for 40 minutes. Uncover, and bake 15 minutes more, or until hot and bubbly. Let stand 10 minutes before cutting.

SHRIMP LEMON PEPPER LINGUINI

Servings: 4 - Prep: 15m - Cooks: 25m - Total: 40m

NUTRITION FACTS

Calories: 484, Carbohydrates: 47.7g, Fat: 18.4g, Protein: 31.6g, Cholesterol: 204mg

INGREDIENTS

- 1 (8 ounce) package linguine pasta
- salt to taste
- 1 tablespoon olive oil
- 2 teaspoons freshly ground black pepper
- 6 cloves garlic, minced
- 1 pound fresh shrimp, peeled and deveined
- 1/2 cup chicken broth
- 1/4 cup butter
- 1/4 cup white wine

- 3 tablespoons chopped fresh parsley
- 1 lemon, juiced
- 1 tablespoon chopped fresh basil
- 1/2 teaspoon lemon zest

DIRECTIONS

1. Bring a large pot of lightly salted water to a boil. Add linguine, and cook for 9 to 13 minutes or until al dente; drain.

2. Heat oil in a large saucepan over medium heat, and saute garlic about 1 minute. Mix in chicken broth, wine, lemon juice, lemon zest, salt, and pepper. Reduce heat, and simmer until liquid is reduced by about 1/2.

3. Mix shrimp, butter, parsley, and basil into the saucepan. Cook 2 to 3 minutes, until shrimp is opaque. Stir in the cooked linguine, and continue cooking 2 minutes, until well coated.

EASY TUNA CASSEROLE

Servings: 8 - Prep: 15m - Cooks: 30m - Total: 45m

NUTRITION FACTS

Calories: 462, Carbohydrates: 37.1g, Fat: 28.5g, Protein: 11.5g, Cholesterol: 23mg

INGREDIENTS

- 3 cups cooked macaroni
- 1 cup shredded Cheddar cheese
- 1 (5 ounce) can tuna, drained
- 1 1/2 cups French fried onions
- 1 (10.75 ounce) can condensed cream of chicken soup

DIRECTIONS

1. Preheat oven to 350 degrees F (175 degrees C).

2. In a 9x13-inch baking dish, combine the macaroni, tuna, and soup. Mix well, and then top with cheese.

3. Bake at 350 degrees F (175 degrees C) for about 25 minutes, or until bubbly. Sprinkle with fried onions, and bake for another 5 minutes. Serve hot.

PENNE WITH CHICKEN AND ASPARAGUS

Servings: 8 - Prep: 15m - Cooks: 20m - Total: 35m

NUTRITION FACTS

Calories: 332, Carbohydrates: 43.3g, Fat: 10.9g, Protein: 16.7g, Cholesterol: 20mg

INGREDIENTS

- 1 (16 ounce) package dried penne pasta
- 1/2 cup low-sodium chicken broth
- 5 tablespoons olive oil, divided
- 1 bunch slender asparagus spears, trimmed, cut on diagonal into 1-inch pieces
- 2 skinless, boneless chicken breast halves - cut into cubes
- 1 clove garlic, thinly sliced
- salt and pepper to taste
- 1/4 cup Parmesan cheese
- garlic powder to taste

DIRECTIONS

1. Bring a large pot of lightly salted water to boil. Add pasta, and cook until al dente, about 8 to 10 minutes. Drain, and set aside.

2. Warm 3 tablespoons olive oil in a large skillet over medium-high heat. Stir in chicken, and season with salt, pepper, and garlic powder. Cook until chicken is cooked through and browned, about 5 minutes. Remove chicken to paper towels.

3. Pour chicken broth into the skillet. Then stir in asparagus, garlic, and a pinch more garlic powder, salt, and pepper. Cover, and steam until the asparagus is just tender, about 5 to 10 minutes. Return chicken to the skillet, and warm through.

4. Stir chicken mixture into pasta, and mix well. Let sit about 5 minutes. Drizzle with 2 tablespoons olive oil, stir again, then sprinkle with Parmesan cheese.

PENNE WITH SPICY VODKA TOMATO CREAM SAUCE

Servings: 8 - Prep: 10m - Cooks: 15m - Total: 25m

NUTRITION FACTS

Calories: 435, Carbohydrates: 52.7g, Fat: 18.4g, Protein: 13.3g, Cholesterol: 29mg

INGREDIENTS

- 1 pound uncooked penne pasta
- 3/4 teaspoon salt
- 1/4 cup extra virgin olive oil
- 2 tablespoons vodka
- 4 cloves garlic, minced
- 1/2 cup heavy whipping cream

- 1/2 teaspoon crushed red pepper flakes
- 1/4 cup chopped fresh parsley
- 1 (28 ounce) can crushed tomatoes
- 2 (3.5 ounce) links sweet Italian sausage

DIRECTIONS

1. Bring a large pot of lightly salted water to a boil. Add pasta and cook for 8 to 10 minutes or until al dente; drain.
2. In large skillet, heat oil over moderate heat. Remove casing from sausage and add to skillet. Cook, breaking up the meat, until brown. Add garlic and red pepper and cook, stirring until garlic is golden brown.
3. Add tomatoes and salt; bring to boil. Reduce heat and simmer 15 minutes.
4. Add vodka and cream and bring to boil. Reduce heat to low and add pasta, toss for 1 minute. Stir in fresh parsley and serve.

TUNA NOODLE CASSEROLE FROM SCRATCH

Servings: 6 - Prep: 30m - Cooks: 45m - Total: 1h15m

NUTRITION FACTS

Calories: 546, Carbohydrates: 39.9g, Fat: 31.2g, Protein: 27.2g, Cholesterol: 121mg

INGREDIENTS

- 1/2 cup butter, divided
- 2 cups milk
- 1 (8 ounce) package uncooked medium egg noodles
- salt and pepper to taste
- 1/2 medium onion, finely chopped
- 2 (5 ounce) cans tuna, drained and flaked
- 1 stalk celery, finely chopped
- 1 cup frozen peas, thawed
- 1 clove garlic, minced
- 3 tablespoons bread crumbs
- 8 ounces button mushrooms, sliced
- 2 tablespoons butter, melted
- 1/4 cup all-purpose flour

- 1 cup shredded Cheddar cheese

DIRECTIONS

1. Preheat oven to 375 degrees F (190 degrees C). Butter a medium baking dish with 1 tablespoon butter.

2. Bring a large pot of lightly salted water to a boil. Add egg noodles, cook for 8 to 10 minutes, until al dente, and drain.

3. Melt 1 tablespoon butter in a skillet over medium-low heat. Stir in the onion, celery, and garlic, and cook 5 minutes, until tender. Increase heat to medium-high, and mix in mushrooms. Continue to cook and stir 5 minutes, or until most of the liquid has evaporated.

4. Melt 4 tablespoons butter in a medium saucepan, and whisk in flour until smooth. Gradually whisk in milk, and continue cooking 5 minutes, until sauce is smooth and slightly thickened. Season with salt and pepper. Stir in tuna, peas, mushroom mixture, and cooked noodles. Transfer to the baking dish. Melt remaining 2 tablespoons butter in a small bowl, mix with bread crumbs, and sprinkle over the casserole. Top with cheese.

5. Bake 25 minutes in the preheated oven, or until bubbly and lightly browned.

MACARONI AND CHEESE

Servings: 6 - Prep: 15m - Cooks: 45m - Total: 1h

NUTRITION FACTS

Calories: 695, Carbohydrates: 72.8g, Fat: 32.3g, Protein: 29.4g, Cholesterol: 95mg

INGREDIENTS

- 1 (16 ounce) package elbow macaroni
- 1 pinch ground nutmeg
- 1/4 cup butter
- 1/4 teaspoon Worcestershire sauce
- 1/4 cup all-purpose flour
- 1 teaspoon salt
- 1/4 teaspoon dried thyme
- 3 cups shredded sharp Cheddar cheese, divided
- 1/4 teaspoon cayenne pepper
- 1 teaspoon Dijon mustard
- 1/8 teaspoon white pepper
- 1/2 cup panko bread crumbs
- 3 cups milk
- 1 tablespoon butter, melted

DIRECTIONS

1. Preheat oven to 400 degrees F (200 degrees C).

2. Fill a large pot with lightly salted water and bring to a rolling boil over high heat. Once the water is boiling, stir in the macaroni, and return to a boil. Cook the pasta uncovered, stirring occasionally, until the pasta is cooked through but still slightly firm, about 8 minutes. Drain well.

3. Melt 1/4 cup butter in a large saucepan over medium heat. When the butter starts to foam and bubble, stir in the flour; cook on medium heat until flour just begins to turn pale yellow, 3 to 4 minutes. Add thyme, cayenne pepper, and white pepper; cook and stir another minute, then whisk in 1 cup of milk until smooth. Pour in remaining milk and whisk again. Bring the sauce just to a simmer.

4. Stir in nutmeg, Worcestershire sauce, and salt; simmer on medium-low heat until thickened, about 8 minutes, whisking often. Turn heat off, then add 2 1/4 cups of Cheddar cheese; stir until melted and combined. Add Dijon mustard.

5. Transfer the macaroni into a casserole dish, then pour in the cheese sauce; stir to thoroughly combine sauce with pasta. Mix panko bread crumbs and 1 tablespoon melted butter in a small bowl, and sprinkle crumbs on top of macaroni and cheese. Sprinkle remaining 3/4 cup of Cheddar cheese on top.

6. Bake in the preheated oven until bread crumbs and Cheddar cheese topping are golden brown, about 20 minutes.

GREEK CHICKEN PASTA

Servings: 6 - Prep: 15m - Cooks: 15m - Total: 30m

NUTRITION FACTS

Calories: 488, Carbohydrates: 70g, Fat: 11.4g, Protein: 32.6g, Cholesterol: 55mg

INGREDIENTS

- 1 (16 ounce) package linguine pasta
- 1/2 cup crumbled feta cheese
- 1/2 cup chopped red onion
- 3 tablespoons chopped fresh parsley
- 1 tablespoon olive oil
- 2 tablespoons lemon juice
- 2 cloves garlic, crushed
- 2 teaspoons dried oregano
- 1 pound skinless, boneless chicken breast meat - cut into bite-size pieces
- salt and pepper to taste
- 1 (14 ounce) can marinated artichoke hearts, drained and chopped

* 2 lemons, wedged, for garnish
* 1 large tomato, chopped

DIRECTIONS

1. Bring a large pot of lightly salted water to a boil. Cook pasta in boiling water until tender yet firm to the bit, 8 to 10 minutes; drain.

2. Heat olive oil in a large skillet over medium-high heat. Add onion and garlic; saute until fragrant, about 2 minutes. Stir in the chicken and cook, stirring occasionally, until chicken is no longer pink in the center and the juices run clear, about 5 to 6 minutes.

3. Reduce heat to medium-low; add artichoke hearts, tomato, feta cheese, parsley, lemon juice, oregano, and cooked pasta. Cook and stir until heated through, about 2 to 3 minutes. Remove from heat, season with salt and pepper, and garnish with lemon wedges.

LINDA'S LASAGNA

Servings: 8 - Prep: 45m - Cooks: 1h45m - Total: 2h30m

NUTRITION FACTS

Calories: 494, Carbohydrates: 38.2g, Fat: 21.8g, Protein: 38.2g, Cholesterol: 105mg

INGREDIENTS

* 1 pound lean ground beef
* 1/4 teaspoon ground black pepper
* 1 onion, chopped
* 1 tablespoon white sugar
* 2 (6 ounce) cans tomato paste
* 12 ounces cottage cheese
* 1 (14.5 ounce) can crushed tomatoes
* 1/2 cup grated Parmesan cheese
* 2 cups water
* 1 egg
* 1 tablespoon dried oregano
* 9 lasagna noodles
* 2 teaspoons garlic powder
* 1 pound shredded mozzarella cheese
* 2 teaspoons salt

DIRECTIONS

1. In a large skillet over medium heat, cook beef until brown. Drain. In another skillet over medium heat, cook onion until translucent. Combine beef and onion in a large saucepan with tomato paste, crushed tomatoes, water, oregano, garlic powder, salt, pepper and sugar. Cook over medium heat until mixture comes to a boil. Reduce heat to low and simmer 1 hour.

2. While sauce is simmering, blend cottage cheese, Parmesan and egg until smooth. Set aside.

3. Bring a large pot of lightly salted water to a boil. Add pasta and cook for 8 to 10 minutes or until al dente; drain.

4. Preheat oven to 350 degrees F (175 degrees C).

5. Spread 1 cup of sauce in the bottom of a 9x13 inch baking dish. Cover sauce with 3 noodles. Cover noodles with one-third of remaining sauce. Top with half the mozzarella. Place another layer of noodles and one of sauce over the mozzarella; top that with the cottage cheese mixture. Top with remaining 3 noodles and remaining sauce.

6. Bake in preheated oven 30 minutes. Sprinkle remaining mozzarella on top and bake 15 minutes more, until golden and bubbly.

CLASSIC GOULASH

Servings: 8 - Prep: 15m - Cooks: 1h5m - Total: 1h20m

NUTRITION FACTS

Calories: 386, Carbohydrates: 34.1g, Fat: 14.6g, Protein: 28.2g, Cholesterol: 74mg

INGREDIENTS

- 2 pounds lean ground beef
- 3 tablespoons soy sauce
- 2 large yellow onions, chopped
- 2 tablespoons dried Italian herb seasoning
- 3 cloves garlic, chopped
- 3 bay leaves
- 3 cups water
- 1 tablespoon seasoned salt, or to taste
- 2 (15 ounce) cans tomato sauce
- 2 cups uncooked elbow macaroni
- 2 (14.5 ounce) cans diced tomatoes

DIRECTIONS

1. Cook and stir the ground beef in a large Dutch oven over medium-high heat, breaking the meat up as it cooks, until the meat is no longer pink and has started to brown, about 10 minutes. Skim off excess fat,

and stir in the onions and garlic. Cook and stir the meat mixture until the onions are translucent, about 10 more minutes.

2. Stir water, tomato sauce, diced tomatoes, soy sauce, Italian seasoning, bay leaves, and seasoned salt into the meat mixture and bring to a boil over medium heat. Reduce heat to low, cover, and simmer 20 minutes, stirring occasionally.

3. Stir macaroni into the mixture, cover, and simmer over low heat until the pasta is tender, about 25 minutes, stirring occasionally. Remove from heat, discard bay leaves, and serve.

SPAGHETTI CARBONARA

Servings: 8 - Prep: 20m - Cooks: 20m - Total: 40m

NUTRITION FACTS

Calories: 444, Carbohydrates: 44.7g, Fat: 21.1g, Protein: 16.4g, Cholesterol: 118mg

INGREDIENTS

- 1 pound spaghetti
- 1/4 cup dry white wine (optional)
- 1 tablespoon olive oil
- 4 eggs
- 8 slices bacon, diced
- 1/2 cup grated Parmesan cheese
- 1 tablespoon olive oil
- 1 pinch salt and black pepper to taste
- 1 onion, chopped
- 2 tablespoons chopped fresh parsley
- 1 clove garlic, minced
- 2 tablespoons grated Parmesan cheese

DIRECTIONS

1. In a large pot of boiling salted water, cook spaghetti pasta until al dente. Drain well. Toss with 1 tablespoon of olive oil, and set aside.

2. Meanwhile in a large skillet, cook chopped bacon until slightly crisp; remove and drain onto paper towels. Reserve 2 tablespoons of bacon fat; add remaining 1 tablespoon olive oil, and heat in reused large skillet. Add chopped onion, and cook over medium heat until onion is translucent. Add minced garlic, and cook 1 minute more. Add wine if desired; cook one more minute.

3. Return cooked bacon to pan; add cooked and drained spaghetti. Toss to coat and heat through, adding more olive oil if it seems dry or is sticking together. Add beaten eggs and cook, tossing constantly with

tongs or large fork until eggs are barely set. Quickly add 1/2 cup Parmesan cheese, and toss again. Add salt and pepper to taste (remember that bacon and Parmesan are very salty).

4. Serve immediately with chopped parsley sprinkled on top, and extra Parmesan cheese at table.

BAKED HOMEMADE MACARONI AND CHEESE

Servings: 6 - Prep: 15m - Cooks: 1h - Total: 1h15m

NUTRITION FACTS

Calories: 810, Carbohydrates: 57.3g, Fat: 49.9g, Protein: 32.4g, Cholesterol: 32.4mg

INGREDIENTS

- 2 1/2 cups elbow macaroni
- 4 cups milk
- 1/4 cup butter
- 1 pound shredded Cheddar cheese
- 1/4 cup all-purpose flour
- 1/4 cup butter, melted
- 1/2 teaspoon salt
- 1 sleeve buttery round crackers, crushed

DIRECTIONS

1. Preheat the oven to 350 degrees F (175 degrees C).
2. Fill a large pot with lightly salted water and bring to a boil over high heat. Stir in the macaroni, and cook uncovered, stirring occasionally, until the pasta has cooked through, but is still firm to the bite, about 8 minutes. Drain well.
3. Melt 1/4 cup butter in a large saucepan over medium heat. Stir in flour and salt. Cook, stirring constantly, for 2 minutes. Whisk in milk and simmer, stirring frequently, until mixture thickens slightly, about 5 minutes.
4. Turn off heat and stir in Cheddar cheese until the cheese is melted. Add the macaroni and stir to coat. Pour the mixture into a 9x13-inch baking dish. Mix the 1/4 remaining cup melted butter and crushed crackers together in a bowl; scatter the cracker mixture evenly over the macaroni mixture.
5. Bake in preheated oven until golden brown on top, about 45 minutes.

YAKISOBA CHICKEN

Servings: 6 - Prep: 15m - Cooks: 15m - Total: 30m

NUTRITION FACTS

Calories: 295, Carbohydrates: 40.7g, Fat: 4.8g, Protein: 26.3g, Cholesterol: 46mg

INGREDIENTS

- 1/2 teaspoon sesame oil
- 1/2 cup soy sauce
- 1 tablespoon canola oil
- 1 onion, sliced lengthwise into eighths
- 2 tablespoons chile paste
- 1/2 medium head cabbage, coarsely chopped
- 2 cloves garlic, chopped
- 2 carrots, coarsely chopped
- 4 skinless, boneless chicken breast halves - cut into 1 inch cubes
- 8 ounces soba noodles, cooked and drained

DIRECTIONS

1. In a large skillet combine sesame oil, canola oil and chili paste; stir-fry 30 seconds. Add garlic and stir fry an additional 30 seconds. Add chicken and 1/4 cup of the soy sauce and stir fry until chicken is no longer pink, about 5 minutes. Remove mixture from pan, set aside, and keep warm.

2. In the emptied pan combine the onion, cabbage, and carrots. Stir-fry until cabbage begins to wilt, 2 to 3 minutes. Stir in the remaining soy sauce, cooked noodles, and the chicken mixture to pan and mix to blend. Serve and enjoy.

THREE CHEESE MANICOTTI

Servings: 6 - Prep: 25m - Cooks: 35m - Total: 1h

NUTRITION FACTS

Calories: 611, Carbohydrates: 64.6g, Fat: 24.1g, Protein: 34g, Cholesterol: 96mg

INGREDIENTS

- 1 (8 ounce) package manicotti shells
- 1 tablespoon minced garlic
- 4 cups shredded mozzarella cheese, divided
- 1 egg
- 2 cups ricotta cheese
- 2 tablespoons dried basil
- 1 cup grated Parmesan cheese, divided
- 2 (26 ounce) jars pasta sauce

DIRECTIONS

1. Bring a large pot of lightly salted water to a boil. Add manicotti and cook for 8 to 10 minutes or until al dente; drain.

2. Preheat oven to 350 degrees F (175 degrees C). Lightly grease a 9x13 inch baking dish.

3. In a bowl, mix 3 cups mozzarella cheese, ricotta cheese, 1/2 cup Parmesan cheese, garlic, egg, and basil. Stuff cooked manicotti with the mixture.

4. Spread about 2 cups pasta sauce over the bottom of the prepared baking dish. Arrange stuffed manicotti in the dish, and cover with remaining sauce. Sprinkle with remaining mozzarella cheese.

5. Bake 15 minutes in the preheated oven. Sprinkle with remaining Parmesan, and continue baking 10 minutes, until mozzarella is melted and bubbly.

LAZYGIRL'S GROUND TURKEY STROGANOFF

Servings: 4 - Prep: 15m - Cooks: 20m - Total: 35m

NUTRITION FACTS

Calories: 463, Carbohydrates: 41.8g, Fat: 19.6g, Protein: 30.5g, Cholesterol: 125mg

INGREDIENTS

- 1 (8 ounce) package uncooked egg noodles
- 1 (10.75 ounce) can condensed cream of mushroom soup
- 1 tablespoon vegetable oil
- 1/2 cup water
- 1 pound ground turkey
- 1 tablespoon paprika
- 1 tablespoon minced onion
- salt to taste
- 1 cube chicken bouillon, crumbled

DIRECTIONS

1. Bring a pot of lightly salted water to a boil. Place the egg noodles in the pot, cook 6 to 8 minutes, until al dente, and drain.

2. Heat the oil in a skillet over medium heat. Place the turkey and onion in the skillet and cook until turkey is evenly brown and onion is tender. Mix in the bouillon.

3. Stir the cream of mushroom soup and water into the skillet. Cook and stir until heated through. Season with paprika and salt. Serve over the cooked egg noodles.

BLT PASTA SALAD

Servings: 10 - Prep: 15m - Cooks: 10m - Total: 3h25m - Additional: 3h

NUTRITION FACTS

Calories: 341, Carbohydrates: 38.2g, Fat: 15.5g, Protein: 12.2g, Cholesterol: 26mg

INGREDIENTS

- 1 (16 ounce) package medium seashell pasta
- 1 small onion, chopped
- 1 pound sliced bacon
- 2 tomatoes, chopped
- 11/2 cups light Ranch-style salad dressing

DIRECTIONS

1. Bring a large pot of lightly salted water to a boil. Add the pasta, and cook until tender, about 8 minutes. Drain, and rinse under cold water to cool.

2. Meanwhile, cook the bacon in a large deep skillet over medium-high heat until browned and crisp. Remove from the pan and drain on paper towels.

3. In a large bowl, stir together the Ranch dressing, onion, and tomatoes. Mix in the cooled pasta. The pasta will absorb some of the dressing, so don't worry if it seems like too much. Refrigerate for several hours or overnight. Crumble bacon over the top just before serving.

ANNA'S AMAZING EASY PLEASY MEATBALLS OVER BUTTERED NOODLES

Servings: 24 - Prep: 15m - Cooks: 3h - Total: 3h15m

NUTRITION FACTS

Calories: 492, Carbohydrates: 38.5g, Fat: 25.5g, Protein: 25.9g, Cholesterol: 148mg

INGREDIENTS

- 2 (10.75 ounce) cans condensed cream of celery soup
- 6 pounds frozen Italian-style meatballs
- 2 (10.5 ounce) cans condensed French onion soup
- 2 (16 ounce) packages uncooked egg noodles
- 1 (16 ounce) container sour cream
- 1/2 cup butter

DIRECTIONS

1. In a large slow cooker, mix together the cream of celery soup, French onion soup, and sour cream. Stir in the meatballs. Cook on high heat for 3-4 hours.

2. Bring a large pot of lightly salted water to a boil. Add pasta and cook for 8 to 10 minutes or until al dente; drain. In a large bowl, toss the pasta with butter. Serve meatballs and sauce over the cooked pasta.

HUSBAND'S DELIGHT

Servings: 6 - Prep: 20m - Cooks: 25m - Total: 45m

NUTRITION FACTS

Calories: 667, Carbohydrates: 41.5g, Fat: 39.7g, Protein: 34.6g, Cholesterol: 172mg

INGREDIENTS

- 10 ounces egg noodles
- 1 1/2 cups sour cream
- 1 1/2 pounds ground beef
- 3 ounces cream cheese
- 1 (14.5 ounce) can peeled and diced tomatoes with juice
- 1/2 onion, chopped
- 1 teaspoon salt
- 1 cup shredded Cheddar cheese
- 1 tablespoon white sugar

DIRECTIONS

1. Preheat oven to 350 degrees F (175 degrees C).

2. Bring a large pot of lightly salted water to a boil. Add pasta and cook for 8 to 10 minutes or until al dente; drain.

3. In a large skillet over medium heat, brown the ground beef. Add the tomatoes with juice, salt and sugar and simmer for 15 minutes.

4. In a separate medium bowl, combine the sour cream, cream cheese and onion and mix well. In a 9x13 inch baking dish, place half of the egg noodles, then all of the meat mixture, then the cream mixture. Top with the remaining noodles and sprinkle with the cheese.

5. Bake at 350 degrees F (175 degrees C) for 25 minutes.

FETTUCCINI CARBONARA

Servings: 6 - Prep: 10m - Cooks: 25m - Total: 35m

NUTRITION FACTS

Calories: 614, Carbohydrates: 64.8g, Fat: g, Protein: 26g, Cholesterol: 166mg

INGREDIENTS

- 5 teaspoons olive oil
- 1 (16 ounce) package fettuccini pasta
- 4 shallots, diced
- 3 egg yolks
- 1 large onion, cut into thin strips
- 1/2 cup heavy cream
- 1 pound bacon, cut into strips
- 3/4 cup shredded Parmesan cheese
- 1 clove garlic, chopped
- salt and pepper to taste

DIRECTIONS

1. Heat olive oil in a large heavy saucepan over medium heat. Saute shallots until softened. Stir in onion and bacon, and cook until bacon is evenly browned. Stir in garlic when bacon is about half done. Remove from heat.

2. Bring a large pot of lightly salted water to a boil. Add pasta and cook for 8 to 10 minutes or until al dente. Drain pasta, then return it to the pot.

3. In a medium bowl, whisk together egg yolks, cream, and shredded Parmesan. Pour the bacon mixture over the pasta, then stir in the cream mixture. Season with salt and pepper.

ANGEL HAIR WITH FETA AND SUN-DRIED TOMATOES

Servings: 8 - Prep: 15m - Cooks: 15m - Total: 30m

NUTRITION FACTS

Calories: 369, Carbohydrates: 39.2g, Fat: 17.5g, Protein: 15.6g, Cholesterol: 34mg

INGREDIENTS

- 1 (16 ounce) package angel hair pasta
- 1 (8 ounce) package tomato basil feta cheese, crumbled
- 1/4 cup olive oil
- 1 cup grated Parmesan cheese
- 4 cloves garlic, crushed
- 1 bunch fresh cilantro, chopped
- 3 ounces sun-dried tomatoes, softened and chopped

- salt and pepper to taste

DIRECTIONS

1. Bring a large pot of lightly salted water to a boil. Cook pasta in boiling water until done; drain. Return pasta to the pot.

2. Mix in olive oil, garlic, tomatoes, feta, and Parmesan cheese. Stir in cilantro and season with salt and pepper. Serve warm.

RATATOUILLE BAKE

Servings: 6 - Prep: 15m - Cooks: 45m - Total: 1h

NUTRITION FACTS

Calories: 188, Carbohydrates: 22g, Fat: 7.6g, Protein: 9.7g, Cholesterol: 24mg

INGREDIENTS

- 1 tablespoon olive oil
- 1 tablespoon dried basil
- 5 cloves garlic, minced
- 1 tablespoon dried parsley
- 1 onion, chopped
- 1/2 teaspoon salt
- 2 cups peeled and diced eggplant
- 1/8 teaspoon black pepper
- 2 cups chopped zucchini
- 1 (8 ounce) package frozen cheese ravioli
- 1 green bell pepper, chopped
- 3/4 cup shredded mozzarella cheese
- 1 (14.5 ounce) can diced tomatoes

DIRECTIONS

1. Preheat oven to 350 degrees F (175 degrees C); spray a 2 1/2-quart baking dish with cooking spray.

2. Heat the olive oil in a large skillet over medium heat; cook and stir the garlic, onion, and eggplant with the garlic until the vegetables have begun to soften, about 8 minutes. Stir in the zucchini, bell pepper, tomatoes, basil, parsley, salt, and black pepper; bring the mixture to a boil, stirring frequently. Reduce heat to medium-low and simmer until the vegetables are tender, about 20 minutes.

3. Cook the frozen ravioli as directed on the package; drain. Spread the cooked ravioli in a layer into the bottom of the prepared baking dish; spoon the hot vegetables over the ravioli. Sprinkle with the cheese.

4. Bake in the preheated oven until the casserole is bubbling and the cheese is melted, about 20 minutes.

PESTO CHICKEN FLORENTINE

Servings: 4 - Prep: 20m - Cooks: 35m - Total: 55m

NUTRITION FACTS

Calories: 572, Carbohydrates: 57.3g, Fat: 19.3g, Protein: 41.9g, Cholesterol: 84mg

INGREDIENTS

- 2 tablespoons olive oil
- 1 (4.5 ounce) package dry Alfredo sauce mix
- 2 cloves garlic, finely chopped
- 2 tablespoons pesto
- 4 skinless, boneless chicken breast halves - cut into strips
- 1 (8 ounce) package dry penne pasta
- 2 cups fresh spinach leaves
- 1 tablespoon grated Romano cheese

DIRECTIONS

1. Heat oil in a large skillet over medium high heat. Add garlic, saute for 1 minute; then add chicken and cook for 7 to 8 minutes on each side. When chicken is close to being cooked through (no longer pink inside), add spinach and saute all together for 3 to 4 minutes.

2. Meanwhile, prepare Alfredo sauce according to package directions. When finished, stir in 2 tablespoons pesto; set aside.

3. In a large pot of salted boiling water, cook pasta for 8 to 10 minutes or until al dente. Rinse under cold water and drain.

4. Add chicken/spinach mixture to pasta, then stir in pesto/Alfredo sauce. Mix well, top with cheese and serve.

GRANDMA'S CHICKEN NOODLE SOUP

Servings: 12 - Prep: 20m - Cooks: 25m - Total: 45m

NUTRITION FACTS

Calories: 147, Carbohydrates: 11.4g, Fat: 3.6g, Protein: 15.7g, Cholesterol: 33mg

INGREDIENTS

- 2 1/2 cups wide egg noodles
- 1 cup chopped celery
- 1 teaspoon vegetable oil
- 1 cup chopped onion

- 12 cups chicken broth
- 1/3 cup cornstarch
- 1 1/2 tablespoons salt
- 1/4 cup water
- 1 teaspoon poultry seasoning
- 3 cups diced, cooked chicken meat

DIRECTIONS

1. Bring a large pot of lightly salted water to a boil. Add egg noodles and oil, and boil for 8 minutes, or until tender. Drain, and rinse under cool running water.

2. In a large saucepan or Dutch oven, combine broth, salt, and poultry seasoning. Bring to a boil. Stir in celery and onion. Reduce heat, cover, and simmer 15 minutes.

3. In a small bowl, mix cornstarch and water together until cornstarch is completely dissolved. Gradually add to soup, stirring constantly. Stir in noodles and chicken, and heat through.

CHICKEN FETTUCCINI ALFREDO

Servings: 8 - Prep: 30m - Cooks: 30m - Total: 1h

NUTRITION FACTS

Calories: 673, Carbohydrates: 57g, Fat: 30.8g, Protein: 43.3g, Cholesterol: 133mg

INGREDIENTS

- 6 skinless, boneless chicken breast halves - cut into cubes
- 1 tablespoon salt
- 6 tablespoons butter, divided
- 3/4 teaspoon ground white pepper
- 4 cloves garlic, minced, divided
- 3 cups milk
- 1 tablespoon Italian seasoning
- 1 cup half-and-half
- 1 pound fettuccini pasta
- 3/4 cup grated Parmesan cheese
- 1 onion, diced
- 8 ounces shredded Colby-Monterey Jack cheese
- 1 (8 ounce) package sliced mushrooms
- 3 roma (plum) tomatoes, diced
- 1/3 cup all-purpose flour

- 1/2 cup sour cream

DIRECTIONS

1. In a large skillet over medium heat combine chicken, 2 tablespoons butter, 2 cloves garlic, and Italian seasoning. Cook until chicken is no longer pink inside. Remove from skillet and set aside.

2. Bring a large pot of lightly salted water to a boil. Add pasta and cook for 8 to 10 minutes or until al dente; drain.

3. Meanwhile, melt 4 tablespoons butter in the skillet. Saute onion, 2 cloves garlic, and mushrooms until onions are transparent. Stir in flour, salt and pepper; cook 2 minutes. Slowly add milk and half-and-half, stirring until smooth and creamy. Stir in Parmesan and Colby-Monterey Jack cheeses; stir until cheese is melted. Stir in chicken mixture, tomatoes and sour cream. Serve over cooked fettuccini.

BEEF TIPS AND NOODLES

Servings: 8 - Prep: 10m - Cooks: 1h - Total: 1h15m - Additional: 5m

NUTRITION FACTS

Calories: 314, Carbohydrates: 41.1g, Fat: 8.8g, Protein: 17.4g, Cholesterol: 65mg

INGREDIENTS

- 1 pound sirloin tips, cubed
- 1 (4.5 ounce) can mushrooms, drained
- 1 (10.75 ounce) can condensed cream of mushroom soup
- 1 cup water
- 1 (1.25 ounce) package beef with onion soup mix
- 1 (16 ounce) package wide egg noodles

DIRECTIONS

1. Preheat oven to 400 degrees F (200 degrees C).

2. In a 13x9 inch casserole dish, combine the mushroom and beef onion soups, canned mushrooms and water. Mix thoroughly and add beef tips. Turn to coat well.

3. Bake in a preheated oven for 1 hour.

4. While beef tips are baking, bring a large pot of lightly salted water to a boil. Add pasta and cook for 8 to 10 minutes or until al dente; drain. Serve beef tips and sauce over noodles.

BLACK BEAN AND COUSCOUS SALAD

Servings: 8 - Prep: 30m - Cooks: 5m - Total: 35m

NUTRITION FACTS

Calories: 253, Carbohydrates: 41.1g, Fat: 5.8g, Protein: 10.3g, Cholesterol: 0mg

INGREDIENTS

- 1 cup uncooked couscous
- 8 green onions, chopped
- 1 1/4 cups chicken broth
- 1 red bell pepper, seeded and chopped
- 3 tablespoons extra virgin olive oil
- 1/4 cup chopped fresh cilantro
- 2 tablespoons fresh lime juice
- 1 cup frozen corn kernels, thawed
- 1 teaspoon red wine vinegar
- 2 (15 ounce) cans black beans, drained
- 1/2 teaspoon ground cumin
- salt and pepper to taste

DIRECTIONS

1. Bring chicken broth to a boil in a 2 quart or larger sauce pan and stir in the couscous. Cover the pot and remove from heat. Let stand for 5 minutes.
2. In a large bowl, whisk together the olive oil, lime juice, vinegar and cumin. Add green onions, red pepper, cilantro, corn and beans and toss to coat.
3. Fluff the couscous well, breaking up any chunks. Add to the bowl with the vegetables and mix well. Season with salt and pepper to taste and serve at once or refrigerate until ready to serve.

CREAMY PESTO SHRIMP

Servings: 8 - Prep: 15m - Cooks: 15m - Total: 30m

NUTRITION FACTS

Calories: 646, Carbohydrates: 43g, Fat: 42.5g, Protein: 23.1g, Cholesterol: 210mg

INGREDIENTS

- 1 pound linguine pasta
- 1 cup grated Parmesan cheese
- 1/2 cup butter
- 1/3 cup pesto
- 2 cups heavy cream
- 1 pound large shrimp, peeled and deveined
- 1/2 teaspoon ground black pepper

DIRECTIONS

1. Bring a large pot of lightly salted water to a boil. Add linguine pasta, and cook for 8 to 10 minutes, or until al dente; drain.

2. In a large skillet, melt the butter over medium heat. Stir in cream, and season with pepper. Cook 6 to 8 minutes, stirring constantly.

3. Stir Parmesan cheese into cream sauce, stirring until thoroughly mixed. Blend in the pesto, and cook for 3 to 5 minutes, until thickened.

4. Stir in the shrimp, and cook until they turn pink, about 5 minutes. Serve over the hot linguine.

BASIL CHICKEN OVER ANGEL HAIR

Servings: 4 - Prep: 15m - Cooks: 20m - Total: 35m

NUTRITION FACTS

Calories: 362, Carbohydrates: 37.8g, Fat: 10.8g, Protein: 28.4g, Cholesterol: 57mg

INGREDIENTS

- 1 (8 ounce) package angel hair pasta
- 2 cups boneless chicken breast halves, cooked and cubed
- 2 teaspoons olive oil
- 1/4 cup chopped fresh basil
- 1/2 cup finely chopped onion
- 1/2 teaspoon salt
- 1 clove garlic, chopped
- 1/8 teaspoon hot pepper sauce
- 2 1/2 cups chopped tomatoes
- 1/4 cup Parmesan cheese

DIRECTIONS

1. In a large pot of salted boiling water, cook angel hair pasta until it is al dente, about 8 to 10 minutes. Drain, and set aside.

2. In a large skillet, heat oil over medium-high heat. Saute the onions and garlic. Stir in the tomatoes, chicken, basil, salt and hot pepper sauce. Reduce heat to medium, and cover skillet. Simmer for about 5 minutes, stirring frequently, until mixture is hot and tomatoes are soft.

3. Toss sauce with hot cooked angel hair pasta to coat. Serve with Parmesan cheese.

SESAME PASTA CHICKEN SALAD

Servings: 10 - Prep: 20m - Cooks: 10m - Total: 30m

NUTRITION FACTS

Calories: 349, Carbohydrates: 38.3g, Fat: 15.2g, Protein: 15.9g, Cholesterol: 24mg

INGREDIENTS

- 1/4 cup sesame seeds
- 1/2 teaspoon ground ginger
- 1 (16 ounce) package bow tie pasta
- 1/4 teaspoon ground black pepper
- 1/2 cup vegetable oil
- 3 cups shredded, cooked chicken breast meat
- 1/3 cup light soy sauce
- 1/3 cup chopped fresh cilantro
- 1/3 cup rice vinegar
- 1/3 cup chopped green onion
- 1 teaspoon sesame oil
- 3 tablespoons white sugar

DIRECTIONS

1. Heat a skillet over medium-high heat. Add sesame seeds, and cook stirring frequently until lightly toasted. Remove from heat, and set aside.
2. Bring a large pot of lightly salted water to a boil. Add pasta, and cook for 8 to 10 minutes, or until al dente. Drain pasta, and rinse under cold water until cool. Transfer to a large bowl.
3. In a jar with a tight-fitting lid, combine vegetable oil, soy sauce, vinegar, sesame oil, sugar, sesame seeds, ginger, and pepper. Shake well.
4. Pour sesame dressing over pasta, and toss to coat evenly. Gently mix in chicken, cilantro, and green onions.

BAKED ZITI

Servings: 8 - Prep: 20m - Cooks: 30m - Total: 50m

NUTRITION FACTS

Calories: 761, Carbohydrates: 74.9g, Fat: 34.4g, Protein: 36.2g, Cholesterol: 96mg

INGREDIENTS

- 1 (16 ounce) package dry ziti pasta
- 6 ounces sliced mozzarella cheese
- 1 pound lean ground beef
- 1 1/2 cups sour cream
- 1 onion, chopped

- 1/2 cup grated Parmesan cheese
- 2 (28 ounce) jars spaghetti sauce
- 1/4 cup chopped fresh basil
- 6 ounces sliced provolone cheese

DIRECTIONS

1. Bring a large pot of lightly salted water to a boil. Add pasta and cook for 8 to 10 minutes or until al dente; drain.
2. In a large skillet, brown beef over medium heat. Add onions; saute until tender. Drain off fat and add spaghetti sauce; simmer for about 15 minutes.
3. Preheat oven to 350 degrees F (175 degrees C).
4. In a lightly greased 2 quart baking dish, place about half of the pasta; top with a layer of provolone and mozzarella cheese slices. Spread on a layer of half the spaghetti sauce mixture and sour cream.
5. Cover with remaining pasta, cheese and sauce; sprinkle a layer of Parmesan cheese and fresh basil.
6. Bake in preheated oven for about 30 minutes or until cheese and sauce are bubbly; serve.

AMISH MACARONI SALAD

Servings: 6 - Prep: 15m - Cooks: 10m - Total: 1h25m

NUTRITION FACTS

Calories: 532, Carbohydrates: 66g, Fat: 25.3g, Protein: 9g, Cholesterol: 133mg

INGREDIENTS

- 2 cups uncooked elbow macaroni
- 2 cups creamy salad dressing (e.g. Miracle Whip)
- 3 hard-cooked eggs, chopped
- 3 tablespoons prepared yellow mustard
- 1 small onion, chopped
- 3/4 cup white sugar
- 3 stalks celery, chopped
- 2 1/4 teaspoons white vinegar
- 1 small red bell pepper, seeded and chopped
- 1/4 teaspoon salt
- 2 tablespoons dill pickle relish
- 3/4 teaspoon celery seed

DIRECTIONS

1. Bring a pot of lightly salted water to a boil. Add macaroni, and cook for 8 to 10 minutes, until tender. Drain, and set aside to cool.

2. In a large bowl, stir together the eggs, onion, celery, red pepper, and relish. In a small bowl, stir together the salad dressing, mustard, white sugar, vinegar, salt and celery seed. Pour over the vegetables, and stir in macaroni until well blended. Cover and chill for at least 1 hour before serving.

MOUSE'S MACARONI AND CHEESE

Servings: 6 - Prep: 15m - Cooks: 35m - Total: 50m

NUTRITION FACTS

Calories: 463, Carbohydrates: 34.2g, Fat: 25.9g, Protein: 23g, Cholesterol: 78mg

INGREDIENTS

1 1/2 cups uncooked elbow macaroni

2 cups milk

1/4 cup butter

8 ounces American cheese, cubed

2 tablespoons all-purpose flour

8 ounces processed cheese food (eg. Velveeta), cubed

1 teaspoon mustard powder

1/4 cup seasoned dry bread crumbs

1 teaspoon ground black pepper

DIRECTIONS

1. Preheat oven to 400 degrees F (205 degrees C). Butter a 1 1/2 quart casserole dish. Bring a saucepan of lightly salted water to a boil. Add macaroni, and cook until not quite done, about 6 minutes. Drain.

2. In a separate saucepan, melt the butter over medium heat. Blend in the flour, mustard powder, and pepper until smooth. Slowly stir in the milk, beating out any lumps. Add the American and processed cheeses, and stir constantly until the sauce is thick and smooth.

3. Drain noodles, and stir them into the cheese sauce. Transfer the mixture to the prepared casserole dish. Sprinkle bread crumbs over the top.

4. Cover the dish, and bake for 20 to 25 minutes, or until sauce is thick and bubbly.

BAKED SPAGHETTI

Servings: 8 - Prep: 25m - Cooks: 1h - Total: 1h25m

NUTRITION FACTS

Calories: 728, Carbohydrates: 61.9g, Fat: 33.6g, Protein: 42.5g, Cholesterol: 150mg

INGREDIENTS

- 1 (16 ounce) package spaghetti
- 2 eggs
- 1 pound ground beef
- 1/3 cup grated Parmesan cheese
- 1 onion, chopped
- 5 tablespoons butter, melted
- 1 (32 ounce) jar meatless spaghetti sauce
- 2 cups small curd cottage cheese, divided
- 1/2 teaspoon seasoned salt
- 4 cups shredded mozzarella cheese, divided

DIRECTIONS

1. Preheat oven to 350 degrees F (175 degrees C). Lightly grease a 9x13-inch baking dish.
2. Bring a large pot of lightly salted water to a boil. Cook spaghetti in boiling water, stirring occasionally until cooked through but firm to the bite, about 12 minutes. Drain.
3. Heat a large skillet over medium heat; cook and stir beef and onion until meat is browned and onions are soft and translucent, about 7 minutes. Drain. Stir in spaghetti sauce and seasoned salt.
4. Whisk eggs, Parmesan cheese, and butter in a large bowl. Mix in spaghetti to egg mixture and toss to coat. Place half the spaghetti mixture into baking dish. Top with half the cottage cheese, mozzarella, and meat sauce. Repeat layers. Cover with aluminum foil.
5. Bake in preheated oven for 40 minutes. Remove foil and continue to bake until the cheese is melted and lightly browned, 20 to 25 minutes longer.

SUKI'S SPINACH AND FETA PASTA

Servings: 4 - Prep: 25m - Cooks: 15m - Total: 40m

NUTRITION FACTS

Calories: 451, Carbohydrates: 51.8g, Fat: 20.6g, Protein: 17.8g, Cholesterol: 50mg

INGREDIENTS

- 1 (8 ounce) package penne pasta
- 1 cup sliced fresh mushrooms
- 2 tablespoons olive oil
- 2 cups spinach leaves, packed
- 1/2 cup chopped onion
- salt and pepper to taste
- 1 clove garlic, minced

- 1 pinch red pepper flakes
- 3 cups chopped tomatoes
- 8 ounces feta cheese, crumbled

DIRECTIONS

1. Bring a large pot of lightly salted water to a boil. Cook pasta in boiling water until al dente; drain.

2. Meanwhile, heat olive oil in a large skillet over medium-high heat; add onion and garlic, and cook until golden brown. Mix in tomatoes, mushrooms, and spinach. Season with salt, pepper, and red pepper flakes. Cook 2 minutes more, until tomatoes are heated through and spinach is wilted. Reduce heat to medium, stir in pasta and feta cheese, and cook until heated through.

BAKED ZITI

Servings: 12 - Prep: 30m - Cooks: 1h - Total: 1h30m

NUTRITION FACTS

Calories: 489, Carbohydrates: 43.8g, Fat: 24.5g, Protein: 22.1g, Cholesterol: 55mg

INGREDIENTS

- 1 pound dry ziti pasta
- 1 1/2 (26 ounce) jars spaghetti sauce
- 1 1/2 tablespoons olive oil
- salt to taste
- 1 onion, sliced
- 1 (6 ounce) package provolone cheese, sliced
- 1 teaspoon minced fresh rosemary
- 3/4 cup sour cream
- 4 cloves garlic, chopped
- 3/4 cup cottage cheese
- 1/2 pound ground beef
- 1 (6 ounce) package mozzarella cheese, shredded
- 1/2 pound ground pork sausage
- 2 tablespoons freshly grated Parmesan cheese

DIRECTIONS

1. Bring a large pot of lightly salted water to a boil. Cook pasta in boiling water for 8 to 10 minutes, or until al dente; drain.

2. Meanwhile, heat olive oil in large, heavy skillet over medium heat. Cook onion in oil until tender. Stir in rosemary and garlic. Transfer to a small bowl.

3. Place ground beef and sausage in the skillet. Cook over medium-high heat until evenly brown. Stir in the onion mixture and the spaghetti sauce. Season with salt. Reduce heat to low, and simmer for 10 minutes.

4. Preheat oven to 350 degrees F (175 degrees C). Grease a 9x13 inch baking dish. In the prepared dish, layer 1/2 of the cooked pasta, provolone cheese, sour cream, cottage cheese, and a little less than 1/2 of the meat mixture. Then layer the rest of the pasta, mozzarella cheese, remaining meat mixture, and Parmesan cheese.

5. Bake in the preheated oven for 20 to 30 minutes, or until heated through and cheeses are melted.

PEANUT BUTTER NOODLES

Servings: 4 - Prep: 15m - Cooks: 10m - Total: 25m

NUTRITION FACTS

Calories: 330, Carbohydrates: 46.8g, Fat: 12g, Protein: 10.7g, Cholesterol: 0mg

INGREDIENTS

- 1/2 cup chicken broth
- 2 teaspoons hot chile paste (optional)
- 1 1/2 tablespoons minced fresh ginger root
- 3 cloves garlic, minced
- 3 tablespoons soy sauce
- 8 ounces Udon noodles
- 3 tablespoons peanut butter
- 1/4 cup chopped green onions
- 1 1/2 tablespoons honey
- 1/4 cup chopped peanuts

DIRECTIONS

1. Bring a large pot of water to a boil. Add noodles and cook until tender according to package directions. Drain.

2. Meanwhile, combine chicken broth, ginger, soy sauce, peanut butter, honey, chili paste, and garlic in a small saucepan. Cook over medium heat until peanut butter melts and is heated through. Add noodles, and toss to coat. Garnish with green onions and peanuts.

ANTIPASTO PASTA SALAD

Servings: 12 - Prep: 20m - Cooks: 15m - Total: 1h35m - Additional: 1h

NUTRITION FACTS

Calories: 451, Carbohydrates: 33.2g, Fat: 29.1g, Protein: 15g, Cholesterol: 37mg

INGREDIENTS

- 1 pound seashell pasta
- 1 (.7 ounce) package dry Italian-style salad dressing mix
- 1/4 pound Genoa salami, chopped
- 3/4 cup extra virgin olive oil
- 1/4 pound pepperoni sausage, chopped
- 1/4 cup balsamic vinegar
- 1/2 pound Asiago cheese, diced
- 2 tablespoons dried oregano
- 1 (6 ounce) can black olives, drained and chopped
- 1 tablespoon dried parsley
- 1 red bell pepper, diced
- 1 tablespoon grated Parmesan cheese
- 1 green bell pepper, chopped
- salt and ground black pepper to taste
- 3 tomatoes, chopped

DIRECTIONS

1. Cook the pasta in a large pot of salted boiling water until al dente. Drain, and cool under cold water.

2. In a large bowl, combine the pasta, salami, pepperoni, Asiago cheese, black olives, red bell pepper, green bell pepper and tomatoes. Stir in the envelope of dressing mix. Cover, and refrigerate for at least one hour.

3. To prepare the dressing, whisk together the olive oil, balsamic vinegar, oregano, parsley, Parmesan cheese, salt and pepper. Just before serving, pour dressing over the salad, and mix well.

BACON RANCH PASTA SALAD

Servings: 10 - Prep: 10m - Cooks: 15m - Total: 1h25m - Additional: 1h

NUTRITION FACTS

Calories: 336, Carbohydrates: 14.9g, Fat: 26.8g, Protein: 9.3g, Cholesterol: 31mg

INGREDIENTS

- 1 (12 ounce) package uncooked tri-color rotini pasta
- 1/2 teaspoon garlic pepper
- 10 slices bacon
- 1/2 cup milk, or as needed
- 1 cup mayonnaise

- 1 large tomato, chopped

- 3 tablespoons dry ranch salad dressing mix

- 1 (4.25 ounce) can sliced black olives

- 1/4 teaspoon garlic powder

- 1 cup shredded sharp Cheddar cheese

DIRECTIONS

1. Bring a large pot of lightly salted water to a boil; cook rotini at a boil until tender yet firm to the bite, about 8 minutes; drain.

2. Place bacon in a skillet over medium-high heat and cook until evenly brown. Drain and chop.

3. In a large bowl, mix mayonnaise, ranch dressing mix, garlic powder, and garlic pepper. Stir in milk until smooth. Place rotini, bacon, tomato, black olives and cheese in bowl and toss to coat with dressing. Cover and chill at least 1 hour in the refrigerator. Toss with additional milk if the salad seems a little dry.

ANGEL HAIR PASTA WITH SHRIMP AND BASIL

Servings: 4 - Prep: 10m - Cooks: 25m - Total: 35m

NUTRITION FACTS

Calories: 527, Carbohydrates: 46.7g, Fat: 18.1g, Protein: 34g, Cholesterol: 176mg

INGREDIENTS

- 1/4 cup olive oil, divided

- 1/2 cup dry white wine

- 1 (8 ounce) package angel hair pasta

- 1/4 cup chopped parsley

- 1 teaspoon chopped garlic

- 3 tablespoons chopped fresh basil

- 1 pound large shrimp - peeled and deveined

- 3 tablespoons freshly grated Parmesan cheese

- 2 (28 ounce) cans Italian-style diced tomatoes, drained

DIRECTIONS

1. Bring a large pot of water to a boil, and add 1 tablespoon oil. Cook pasta in boiling water until al dente. Place pasta in a colander, and give it a quick rinse with cold water.

2. Heat remaining olive oil in a 10 inch skillet over medium heat. Cook garlic, stirring constantly, until the garlic is tender, about 1 minute. Do not let the garlic burn. Add shrimp, and cook for 3 to 5 minutes. Remove shrimp from the skillet, and set aside.

3. Stir tomatoes, wine, parsley, and basil into the skillet. Continue cooking, stirring occasionally, until liquid is reduced by half, 8 to 12 minutes. Add shrimp, and continue cooking until the shrimp are heated through, about 2 to 3 minutes. Serve the shrimp mixture over the pasta. Sprinkle with Parmesan cheese.

PASTA POMODORO

Servings: 4 - Prep: 15m - Cooks: 15m - Total: 30m

NUTRITION FACTS

Calories: 500, Carbohydrates: 69.7g, Fat: 18.3g, Protein: 16.2g, Cholesterol: 6mg

INGREDIENTS

- 1 (16 ounce) package angel hair pasta
- 1 (10.75 ounce) can low-sodium chicken broth
- 1/4 cup olive oil
- crushed red pepper to taste
- 1/2 onion, chopped
- freshly ground black pepper to taste
- 4 cloves garlic, minced
- 2 tablespoons chopped fresh basil
- 2 cups roma (plum) tomatoes, diced
- 1/4 cup grated Parmesan cheese
- 2 tablespoons balsamic vinegar

DIRECTIONS

1. Bring a large pot of lightly salted water to a boil. Add pasta and cook for 8 minutes or until al dente; drain.

2. Pour olive oil in a large deep skillet over high-heat. Saute onions and garlic until lightly browned. Reduce heat to medium-high and add tomatoes, vinegar and chicken broth; simmer for about 8 minutes.

3. Stir in red pepper, black pepper, basil and cooked pasta, tossing thoroughly with sauce. Simmer for about 5 more minutes and serve topped with grated cheese.

BROOKLYN GIRL'S PENNE ARRABIATA

Servings: 6 - Prep: 20m - Cooks: 25m - Total: 45m

NUTRITION FACTS

Calories: 588, Carbohydrates: 75.3g, Fat: 16.5g, Protein: 33.6g, Cholesterol: 108mg

INGREDIENTS

- 1/2 cup olive oil, divided
- 2 eggs
- 6 cloves garlic, sliced
- 2 cups bread crumbs
- 1 teaspoon red pepper flakes
- 1 teaspoon garlic powder
- 1 (28 ounce) can diced tomatoes with garlic and olive oil
- 1 teaspoon salt
- 1/2 cup tomato sauce
- 1 teaspoon pepper
- 1 bunch fresh basil, chopped
- 1 pound thin chicken breast cutlets

DIRECTIONS

1. Heat 1/4 cup of olive oil in a large skillet over medium heat. Add the garlic, and saute for a few minutes. Sprinkle in the red pepper flakes, and saute for another minute. Pour in the diced tomatoes and tomato sauce, and add the basil. Simmer for about 20 minutes, stirring occasionally.

2. Meanwhile, bring a large pot of lightly salted water to a boil. Add penne pasta, and cook for 8 minutes, or until tender. Drain.

3. In a small bowl, whisk eggs with a fork. Place bread crumbs in a separate bowl. Stir the garlic powder, salt and pepper into the bread crumbs. Dip chicken cutlets into the egg, then press into the bread crumbs until completely coated.

4. Heat remaining olive oil in a large skillet over medium heat. Fry chicken for about 5 minutes per side, or until the coating is a nice dark brown color.

5. Remove chicken, and cut into slices. Toss the chicken slices into the sauce, and simmer for about 10 minutes. Stir in the cooked penne, simmer for a few more minutes to soak up the flavor, then serve.

SHRIMP SCAMPI

Servings: 4 - Prep: 15m - Cooks: 10m - Total: 25m

NUTRITION FACTS

Calories: 606, Carbohydrates: 35.5g, Fat: 30.8g, Protein: 35.3g, Cholesterol: 247mg

INGREDIENTS

- 1 (8 ounce) package angel hair pasta

- 1 cup dry white wine
- 1/2 cup butter
- 1/4 teaspoon ground black pepper
- 4 cloves minced garlic
- 3/4 cup grated Parmesan cheese
- 1 pound shrimp, peeled and deveined
- 1 tablespoon chopped fresh parsley

DIRECTIONS

1. Bring a large pot of salted water to a boil. Stir in pasta and return pot to boil. Cook until al dente. Drain well.
2. Melt butter in a large saucepan over medium heat. Stir in garlic and shrimp. Cook, stirring constantly, for 3 to 5 minutes.
3. Stir in wine and pepper. Bring to a boil and cook for 30 seconds while stirring constantly.
4. Mix shrimp with drained pasta in a serving bowl. Sprinkle with cheese and parsley. Serve immediately.

FETTUCCINE WITH SWEET PEPPER-CAYENNE SAUCE

Servings: 4 - Prep: 5m - Cooks: 10m - Total: 15m

NUTRITION FACTS

Calories: 475, Carbohydrates: 69.3g, Fat: 13.9g, Protein: 20.3g, Cholesterol: 37mg

INGREDIENTS

- 12 ounces dry fettuccine pasta
- 1 cup reduced fat sour cream
- 2 red bell peppers, julienned
- 3/4 cup chicken broth
- 3 cloves garlic, minced
- 3/4 cup grated Parmesan cheese
- 3/4 teaspoon cayenne pepper
- salt and pepper to taste

DIRECTIONS

1. Bring a large pot of lightly salted water to a boil. Add pasta and cook for 8 to 10 minutes or until al dente; drain.

2. Meanwhile, spray cooking oil in a large skillet and saute red bell peppers, garlic and cayenne pepper over medium heat for 3 to 5 minutes.

3. Stir in sour cream and broth; simmer uncovered for 5 minutes. Remove from heat and stir in cheese.

4. Toss hot pasta with sauce and season with salt and pepper to taste; serve.

SIMPLE HAMBURGER STROGANOFF

Servings: 6 - Prep: 20m - Cooks: 10m - Total: 30m

NUTRITION FACTS

Calories: 735, Carbohydrates: 60.9g, Fat: 42g, Protein: 28.9g, Cholesterol: 159mg

INGREDIENTS

- 1 (16 ounce) package egg noodles
- 1 (6 ounce) can chopped mushrooms, with liquid
- 1 pound lean ground beef
- 1/2 cup milk
- 1 (.75 ounce) packet dry brown gravy mix
- 1 (8 ounce) container sour cream
- 1 (8 ounce) package cream cheese
- 2 (10.75 ounce) cans condensed cream of mushroom soup

DIRECTIONS

1. Bring a large pot of lightly salted water to a boil. Add egg noodles and cook for 8 to 10 minutes or until al dente; drain.

2. In a skillet over medium heat, brown the ground beef until no pink shows, about 5 minutes; drain fat.

3. Mix brown gravy, cream cheese, and mushrooms with hamburger, stirring until cream cheese melts. Add milk, sour cream, and mushroom soup to cooked pasta. Blend hamburger mixture with pasta.

SHRIMP AND MUSHROOM LINGUINI WITH CREAMY CHEESE HERB SAUCE

Servings: 4 - Prep: 15m - Cooks: 15m - Total: 30m

NUTRITION FACTS

Calories: 601, Carbohydrates: 44g, Fat: 38.3g, Protein: 23.2g, Cholesterol: 210mg

INGREDIENTS

- 1 (8 ounce) package linguini pasta
- 1 (3 ounce) package cream cheese

- 2 tablespoons butter

- 2 tablespoons chopped fresh parsley

- 1/2 pound fresh mushrooms, sliced

- 3/4 teaspoon dried basil

- 1/2 cup butter

- 2/3 cup boiling water

- 2 cloves garlic, minced

- 1/2 pound cooked shrimp

DIRECTIONS

1. Bring a large pot of lightly salted water to a boil. Add linguini and cook until tender, about 7 minutes. Drain.

2. Meanwhile, heat 2 tablespoons butter in a large skillet over medium-high heat. Add mushrooms; cook and stir until tender. Transfer to a plate.

3. In the same pan, melt 1/2 cup butter with the minced garlic. Stir in the cream cheese, breaking it up with a spoon as it melts. Stir in the parsley and basil. Simmer for 5 minutes. Mix in boiling water until sauce is smooth. Stir in cooked shrimp and mushrooms; heat sauce through.

4. Toss linguini with shrimp sauce and serve.

CHICKEN AND GNOCCHI SOUP

Servings: 6 - Prep: 20m - Cooks: 20m - Total: 40m

NUTRITION FACTS

Calories: 389, Carbohydrates: 23.9g, Fat: 20.1g, Protein: 29.8g, Cholesterol: 112mg

INGREDIENTS

- 1 tablespoon olive oil

- 1 (16 ounce) package mini potato gnocchi

- 1 small onion, diced

- 1 (6 ounce) bag baby spinach leaves

- 3 stalks celery, diced

- 1 tablespoon cornstarch (optional)

- 3 cloves garlic, minced

- 2 tablespoons cold water (optional)

- 2 carrots, shredded

- 2 cups half-and-half cream

- 1 pound cooked, cubed chicken breast

- salt and ground black pepper to taste
- 4 cups chicken broth

DIRECTIONS

1. Heat olive oil in a large pot over medium heat. Cook onion, celery, garlic, and carrots in the hot oil until onion is translucent, about 5 minutes. Stir in cubed chicken and chicken broth; bring to a simmer.

2. Stir gnocchi into the simmering soup and cook until they begin to float, 3 to 4 minutes. Stir in spinach; cook until wilted, about 3 additional minutes.

3. Whisk cornstarch into cold water until smooth. Stir cornstarch mixture and half-and-half into simmering soup. Cook until soup thickens slightly, about 5 minutes. Season to taste with salt and black pepper.

MOM'S FAVORITE BAKED MAC AND CHEESE

Servings: 6 - Prep: 10m - Cooks: 45m - Total: 1h5m - Additional: 10m

NUTRITION FACTS

Calories: 561, Carbohydrates: 36.5g, Fat: 33.3g, Protein: 28.3g, Cholesterol: 100mg

INGREDIENTS

- 2 tablespoons butter
- 1/2 teaspoon dry mustard
- 1/4 cup finely chopped onion
- 1/4 teaspoon ground black pepper
- 2 tablespoons all-purpose flour
- 1 (8 ounce) package elbow macaroni
- 2 cups milk
- 2 cups shredded sharp Cheddar cheese
- 3/4 teaspoon salt
- 1 (8 ounce) package processed American cheese, cut into strips

DIRECTIONS

1. Preheat oven to 350 degrees F (175 degrees C).

2. Melt butter in a medium saucepan over medium heat. Saute onion for 2 minutes. Stir in flour and cook 1 minute, stirring constantly. Stir in milk, salt, mustard and pepper; cook, stirring frequently, until mixture boils and thickens.

3. Meanwhile, bring a pot of lightly salted water to a boil. Add macaroni and cook for 8 to 10 minutes or until al dente; drain.

4. To the milk mixture add the Cheddar and American cheeses; stir until cheese melts. Combine macaroni and cheese sauce in a 2 quart baking dish; mix well.

5. Bake in preheated oven for 30 minutes, or until hot and bubbly. Let cool 10 minutes before serving.

PENNE PASTA WITH SPINACH AND BACO

Servings: 4 - Prep: 10m - Cooks: 15m - Total: 25m

NUTRITION FACTS

Calories: 517, Carbohydrates: 73.8g, Fat: 14.8g, Protein: 21g, Cholesterol: 15mg

INGREDIENTS

- 1 (12 ounce) package penne pasta
- 2 tablespoons minced garlic
- 2 tablespoons olive oil, divided
- 1 (14.5 ounce) can diced tomatoes
- 6 slices bacon, chopped
- 1 bunch fresh spinach, rinsed and torn into bite-size pieces

DIRECTIONS

1. Bring a large pot of lightly salted water to a boil. Add the penne pasta, and cook until tender, 8 to 10 minutes.

2. Meanwhile, heat 1 tablespoon of olive oil in a skillet over medium heat. Place bacon in the skillet, and cook until browned and crisp. Add garlic, and cook for about 1 minute. Stir in the tomatoes, and cook until heated through.

3. Place the spinach into a colander, and drain the hot pasta over it so it is wilted. Transfer to a large serving bowl, and toss with the remaining olive oil, and the bacon and tomato mixture.

SHRIMP SCAMPI WITH PASTA

Servings: 6 - Prep: 20m - Cooks: 20m - Total: 40m

NUTRITION FACTS

Calories: 511, Carbohydrates: 57.5g, Fat: 19.4g, Protein: 21.9g, Cholesterol: 135mg

INGREDIENTS

- 1 (16 ounce) package linguine pasta
- 1 pinch kosher salt and freshly ground pepper
- 2 tablespoons butter
- 1/2 cup dry white wine
- 2 tablespoons extra-virgin olive oil

- 1 lemon, juiced
- 2 shallots, finely diced
- 2 tablespoons butter
- 2 cloves garlic, minced
- 2 tablespoons extra-virgin olive oil
- 1 pinch red pepper flakes (optional)
- 1/4 cup finely chopped fresh parsley leaves
- 1 pound shrimp, peeled and deveined
- 1 teaspoon extra-virgin olive oil, or to taste

DIRECTIONS

1. Bring a large pot of salted water to a boil; cook linguine in boiling water until nearly tender, 6 to 8 minutes. Drain.

2. Melt 2 tablespoons butter with 2 tablespoons olive oil in a large skillet over medium heat. Cook and stir shallots, garlic, and red pepper flakes in the hot butter and oil until shallots are translucent, 3 to 4 minutes. Season shrimp with kosher salt and black pepper; add to the skillet and cook until pink, stirring occasionally, 2 to 3 minutes. Remove shrimp from skillet and keep warm.

3. Pour white wine and lemon juice into skillet and bring to a boil while scraping the browned bits of food off of the bottom of the skillet with a wooden spoon. Melt 2 tablespoons butter in skillet, stir 2 tablespoons olive oil into butter mixture, and bring to a simmer. Toss linguine, shrimp, and parsley in the butter mixture until coated; season with salt and black pepper. Drizzle with 1 teaspoon olive oil to serve.

GREEK PASTA SALAD

Servings: 4 - Prep: 15m - Cooks: 10m - Total: 2h25m - Additional: 2h

NUTRITION FACTS

Calories: 746, Carbohydrates: 40.4g, Fat: 56.1g, Protein: 22.1g, Cholesterol: 70mg

INGREDIENTS

- 1/2 cup olive oil
- 3 cups fresh sliced mushrooms
- 1/2 cup red wine vinegar
- 15 cherry tomatoes, halved
- 1 1/2 teaspoons garlic powder
- 1 cup sliced red bell peppers
- 11/2 teaspoons dried basil

- 3/4 cup crumbled feta cheese
- 1 1/2 teaspoons dried oregano
- 1/2 cup chopped green onions
- 3/4 teaspoon ground black pepper
- 1 (4 ounce) can whole black olives
- 3/4 teaspoon white sugar
- 3/4 cup sliced pepperoni sausage, cut into strips
- 2 1/2 cups cooked elbow macaroni

DIRECTIONS

1. In a large bowl, whisk together olive oil, vinegar, garlic powder, basil, oregano, black pepper, and sugar. Add cooked pasta, mushrooms, tomatoes, red peppers, feta cheese, green onions, olives, and pepperoni. Toss until evenly coated. Cover, and chill 2 hours or overnight.

EASY LASAGNA

Servings: 12 - Prep: 15m - Cooks: 1h - Total: 1h25m - Additional: 10m

NUTRITION FACTS

Calories: 377, Carbohydrates: 26.4g, Fat: 16.7g, Protein: 29.4g, Cholesterol: 89mg

INGREDIENTS

- 1 pound lean ground beef
- 2 teaspoons dried parsley
- 1 (32 ounce) jar spaghetti sauce
- salt to taste
- 32 ounces cottage cheese
- ground black pepper to taste
- 3 cups shredded mozzarella cheese
- 9 lasagna noodles
- 2 eggs
- 1/2 cup water
- 1/2 cup grated Parmesan cheese

DIRECTIONS

1. In a large skillet over medium heat brown the ground beef. Drain the grease. Add spaghetti sauce and simmer for 5 minutes.

2. In a large bowl, mix together the cottage cheese, 2 cups of the mozzarella cheese, eggs, half of the grated Parmesan cheese, dried parsley, salt and ground black pepper.

3. To assemble, in the bottom of a 9x13 inch baking dish evenly spread 3/4 cup of the sauce mixture. Cover with 3 uncooked lasagna noodles, 1 3/4 cup of the cheese mixture, and 1/4 cup sauce. Repeat layers once more: top with 3 noodles, remaining sauce, remaining mozzarella and Parmesan cheese. Add 1/2 cup water to the edges of the pan. Cover with aluminum foil.

4. Bake in a preheated 350 degree F(175 degrees C) oven for 45 minutes. Uncover and bake an additional 10 minutes. Let stand 10 minutes before serving.

SLOW COOKER LASAGNA

Servings: 10 - Prep: 20m - Cooks: 4h20m - Total: 4h40m

NUTRITION FACTS

Calories: 446, Carbohydrates: 35.7g, Fat: 20.3g, Protein:31.2 g, Cholesterol: 72mg

INGREDIENTS

- 1 pound lean ground beef
- 1 teaspoon dried oregano
- 1 onion, chopped
- 1 (12 ounce) package lasagna noodles
- 2 teaspoons minced garlic
- 12 ounces cottage cheese
- 1 (29 ounce) can tomato sauce
- 1/2 cup grated Parmesan cheese
- 1 (6 ounce) can tomato paste
- 16 ounces shredded mozzarella cheese
- 1 1/2 teaspoons salt

DIRECTIONS

1. In a large skillet over medium heat cook the ground beef, onion, and garlic until brown. Add the tomato sauce, tomato paste, salt, and oregano and stir until well incorporated. Cook until heated through.

2. In a large bowl mix together the cottage cheese, grated Parmesan cheese, and shredded mozzarella cheese.

3. Spoon a layer of the meat mixture onto the bottom of the slow cooker. Add a double layer of the uncooked lasagna noodles. Break to fit noodles into slow cooker. Top noodles with a portion of the cheese mixture. Repeat the layering of sauce, noodles, and cheese until all the ingredients are used.

4. Cover, and cook on low setting for 4 to 6 hours.

STUFFED SHELLS

Servings: 8 - Prep: 25m - Cooks: 25m - Total: 50m

NUTRITION FACTS

Calories: 557, Carbohydrates: 59.6g, Fat: 18.2g, Protein: 37g, Cholesterol: 98mg

INGREDIENTS

- 1 (16 ounce) package jumbo pasta shells
- 1 pinch garlic powder
- 4 cups large curd cottage cheese
- 1 teaspoon dried oregano
- 12 ounces mozzarella cheese, shredded
- 1 teaspoon dried parsley
- 1/2 cup grated Parmesan cheese
- 1 (26 ounce) jar spaghetti sauce
- 2 eggs, lightly beaten
- 1/4 cup grated Parmesan cheese

DIRECTIONS

1. Cook shells according to package directions. Place in cold water to stop cooking. Drain.
2. Mix together cottage cheese, mozzarella cheese, 1/2 cup Parmesan cheese, eggs, and garlic powder. Rub the dried herbs in the palms of your hands to pulverize them, and stir into the cheese mixture. Stuff mixture into the shells.
3. Spread 1/3 of spaghetti sauce in the bottom of a 15 x 10 inch pan. Place shells open side up, and close together in pan. Spread remaining sauce over top, and sprinkle with remaining 1/4 cup Parmesan cheese.
4. Bake at 350 degrees F (175 degrees C) for 25 to 35 minutes, or until bubbly. Let stand 10 minutes before serving.

PESTO PASTA WITH CHICKEN

Servings: 8 - Prep: 10m - Cooks: 20m - Total: 30m

NUTRITION FACTS

Calories: 328, Carbohydrates: 43.3g, Fat: 10.1g, Protein: 17.4g, Cholesterol: 22mg

INGREDIENTS

- 1 (16 ounce) package bow tie pasta
- crushed red pepper flakes to taste
- 1 teaspoon olive oil

- 1/3 cup oil-packed sun-dried tomatoes, drained and cut into strips
- 2 cloves garlic, minced
- 1/2 cup pesto sauce
- 2 boneless skinless chicken breasts, cut into bite-size pieces

DIRECTIONS

1. Bring a large pot of lightly salted water to a boil. Add pasta and cook for 8 to 10 minutes or until al dente; drain.
2. Heat oil in a large skillet over medium heat. Saute garlic until tender, then stir in chicken. Season with red pepper flakes. Cook until chicken is golden, and cooked through.
3. In a large bowl, combine pasta, chicken, sun-dried tomatoes and pesto. Toss to coat evenly.

TACO CASSEROLE

Servings: 10 - Prep: 25m - Cooks: 35m - Total: 1h

NUTRITION FACTS

Calories: 334, Carbohydrates: 28.2g, Fat: 17g, Protein: 15..6g, Cholesterol: 50mg

INGREDIENTS

- 1 pound lean ground beef
- 2 ounces shredded Cheddar cheese
- 8 ounces macaroni
- 2 ounces shredded Monterey Jack cheese
- 1/2 cup chopped onion
- 1 cup crushed tortilla chips
- 1 (10.75 ounce) can condensed tomato soup
- 1/2 cup sour cream (optional)
- 1 (14.5 ounce) can diced tomatoes
- 1/4 cup chopped green onions
- 1 (1.25 ounce) package taco seasoning mix

DIRECTIONS

1. Preheat oven to 350 degrees F (175 degrees C).
2. Cook pasta in a large pot of boiling water until al dente. Drain.
3. In a large skillet, cook and stir ground beef and chopped onion over medium heat until brown. Mix in tomato soup, diced tomatoes, and taco seasoning mix. Stir in pasta.
4. Spoon beef mixture into a 9x13 inch baking dish. Sprinkle crumbled taco chips and grated cheese on top.

5. Bake for 30 to 35 minutes, until the cheese is melted. Serve with chopped green onions and sour cream, if desired.

TACOS IN PASTA SHELLS

Servings: 6 - Prep: 30m - Cooks: 30m - Total: 1h

NUTRITION FACTS

Calories: 735, Carbohydrates: 47.6g, Fat: 44.2g, Protein: 35.7g, Cholesterol: 136mg

INGREDIENTS

- 1 1/4 pounds lean ground beef
- 1 cup taco sauce
- 1 (3 ounce) package cream cheese
- 1 cup shredded Cheddar cheese
- 1 teaspoon salt
- 1 cup shredded Monterey Jack cheese
- 1 teaspoon chili powder
- 1 1/2 cups crushed tortilla chips
- 18 jumbo pasta shells
- 1 cup sour cream
- 2 tablespoons butter, melted

DIRECTIONS

1. In a large skillet, brown beef over medium heat until no longer pink; drain. Add cream cheese, salt and chili powder; mix and simmer for 5 minutes.
2. Meanwhile, bring a large pot of lightly salted water to a boil. Add pasta and cook for 8 to 10 minutes or until al dente; drain. Toss cooked shells in butter.
3. reheat oven to 350 degrees F (175 degrees C).
4. Fill shells with beef mixture and arrange in a 9x13 inch baking dish; pour taco sauce over shells. Cover with foil and bake in preheated oven for 15 minutes.
5. Remove dish from oven and top with Cheddar cheese, Monterey Jack cheese and tortilla chips; return dish to oven to cook for 15 minutes more.
6. Top with sour cream and onions; serve.

SARAH'S RICE PILAF

Servings: 136 - Prep: 10m - Cooks: 35m - Total: 50m - Additional: 5m

NUTRITION FACTS

Calories: 244, Carbohydrates: 40g, Fat: 6.5g, Protein: 5.9g, Cholesterol: 18mg

INGREDIENTS

- 2 tablespoons butter
- 2 cloves garlic, minced
- 1/2 cup orzo pasta
- 1/2 cup uncooked white rice
- 1/2 cup diced onion
- 2 cups chicken broth

DIRECTIONS

1. Melt the butter in a lidded skillet over medium-low heat. Cook and stir orzo pasta until golden brown. Stir in onion and cook until onion becomes translucent, then add garlic and cook for 1 minute. Mix in the rice and chicken broth. Increase heat to high and bring to a boil. Reduce heat to medium-low, cover, and simmer until the rice is tender, and the liquid has been absorbed, 20 to 25 minutes. Remove from heat and let stand for 5 minutes, then fluff with a fork.

TURKEY TETRAZZINI

Servings: 8 - Prep: 20m - Cooks: 1h - Total: 1h20m

NUTRITION FACTS

Calories: 565, Carbohydrates: 51.7g, Fat: 22.1g, Protein: 37.6g, Cholesterol: 105mg

INGREDIENTS

- 1 (16 ounce) package uncooked spaghetti
- 2 cups milk
- 1/2 cup butter
- 1 2/3 cups grated Parmesan cheese
- 1/2 cup all-purpose flour
- 4 cups chopped cooked turkey
- 3 cups chicken broth

DIRECTIONS

1. Preheat oven to 350 degrees F (175 degrees C). Lightly grease a baking dish.
2. Bring a large pot of lightly salted water to a boil. Add spaghetti, and cook for 8 to 10 minutes or until al dente. Drain, and place in the prepared baking dish.
3. Melt butter in a medium saucepan over medium heat. Stir in flour. Mix in chicken broth and milk. Cook and stir until the mixture comes to a boil. Stir in about 1 1/3 cups Parmesan cheese, and remove from heat.

4. Mix chicken broth mixture and turkey with spaghetti. Top with remaining cheese. Bake 1 hour in the preheated oven, until surface is lightly browned.

ONE PAN ORECCHIETTE PASTA

Servings: 2 - Prep: 15m - Cooks: 25m - Total: 40m

NUTRITION FACTS

Calories: 662, Carbohydrates: 46.2g, Fat: 39.1g, Protein: 31.2g, Cholesterol: 60mg

INGREDIENTS

- 2 tablespoons olive oil
- 3 1/2 cups low-sodium chicken broth, divided, or as needed
- 1/2 onion, diced
- 1 1/4 cups orecchiette pasta, or more to taste
- salt to taste
- 1/2 cup roughly chopped arugula, or to taste
- 8 ounces spicy Italian sausages, casings removed
- 1/4 cup finely grated Parmigiano-Reggiano cheese, or to taste

DIRECTIONS

1. Heat olive oil in a large, deep skillet over medium heat. Cook and stir onion with a pinch of salt in hot oil until onion is soft and golden, 5 to 7 minutes. Stir sausage into onions; cook and stir until sausage is broken up and browned, 5 to 7 minutes.

2. Pour 1 1/2 cups chicken broth into sausage mixture and bring to a boil while scraping the browned bits of food off of the bottom of the pan with a wooden spoon. Add orecchiette pasta; cook and stir pasta in hot broth, adding remaining broth when liquid is absorbed, until pasta is cooked through and most of the broth is absorbed, about 15 minutes.

3. Stir arugula into pasta-sausage mixture until arugula wilts. Ladle pasta into bowls and dust with Parmigiano-Reggiano cheese.

LEMON CREAM PASTA WITH CHICKEN

Servings: 4 - Prep: 1h - Cooks: 10m - Total: 1h10m

NUTRITION FACTS

Calories: 519, Carbohydrates: 48.1g, Fat: 24.5g, Protein: 29.8g, Cholesterol: 133mg

INGREDIENTS

- 3 skinless, boneless chicken breast halves
- 1/4 cup fresh lemon juice

- 1 lemon, quartered
- 1 (8 ounce) package rotelle pasta
- 2 teaspoons garlic powder, divided
- 1 cup heavy cream
- 1 teaspoon ground black pepper, divided
- 1 teaspoon grated lemon zest
- 2 (14.5 ounce) cans chicken broth

DIRECTIONS

1. Preheat oven to 350 degrees F (175 degrees C). Place chicken in a lightly greased baking dish. Squeeze lemon over both sides of the chicken breasts and season both sides using 1 1/2 teaspoons garlic powder and 3/4 teaspoon pepper. Bake for 40 minutes, or until juices run clear and chicken is no longer pink inside.

2. Meanwhile, in a large saucepan, season the chicken broth with the remaining 1/2 teaspoon garlic powder and 1/4 teaspoon pepper. Bring to a boil and add lemon juice and pasta. Cook over medium heat, stirring occasionally, until all liquid is absorbed, about 25 minutes.

3. Cut cooked chicken into bite-sized pieces and stir into cooked pasta, along with the cream and lemon zest. Cook, stirring, over low heat for 5 minutes. Remove from heat and let stand 5 minutes. Stir thoroughly before serving.

GARLIC CHICKEN WITH ORZO NOODLES

Servings: 4 - Prep: 15m - Cooks: 15m - Total: 30m

NUTRITION FACTS

Calories: 351, Carbohydrates: 40.4g, Fat: 10.6g, Protein: 22.3g, Cholesterol: 38mg

INGREDIENTS

- 1 cup uncooked orzo pasta
- salt to taste
- 2 tablespoons olive oil
- 1 tablespoon chopped fresh parsley
- 2 cloves garlic
- 2 cups fresh spinach leaves
- 1/4 teaspoon crushed red pepper
- grated Parmesan cheese for topping
- 2 skinless, boneless chicken breast halves - cut into bite-size pieces

DIRECTIONS

1. Bring a large pot of lightly salted water to a boil. Add orzo pasta, cook for 8 to 10 minutes, until al dente, and drain.

2. Heat the oil in a skillet over medium-high heat, and cook the garlic and red pepper 1 minute, until garlic is golden brown. Stir in chicken, season with salt, and cook 2 to 5 minutes, until lightly browned and juices run clear. Reduce heat to medium, and mix in the parsley and cooked orzo. Place spinach in the skillet. Continue cooking 5 minutes, stirring occasionally, until spinach is wilted. Serve topped with Parmesan cheese.

SHRIMP FETTUCCINE ALFREDO

Servings: 6 - Prep: 20m - Cooks: 20m - Total: 40m

NUTRITION FACTS

Calories: 440, Carbohydrates: 57.7g, Fat: 10.6g, Protein: 29.2g, Cholesterol: 172mg

INGREDIENTS

- 1 pound fettuccini pasta
- 1 cup half-and-half
- 1 tablespoon butter
- 6 tablespoons grated Parmesan cheese
- 1 pound cooked shrimp - peeled and deveined
- 1 tablespoon chopped fresh parsley
- 4 cloves garlic, minced
- salt to taste

DIRECTIONS

1. Bring a large pot of lightly salted water to a boil. Add pasta and cook for 8 to 10 minutes or until al dente; drain.

2. In a large skillet, cook and stir shrimp and garlic in the butter for about one minute. Pour in half and half; stir. Sprinkle Parmesan cheese in one tablespoon at a time, stirring constantly. After all Parmesan is added, mix in parsley and salt. Stir frequently making sure it does not boil. Sauce will take a while to thicken.

3. When sauce has thickened, combine with cooked pasta noodles; serve hot.

TURKEY VEGGIE MEATLOAF CUPS

Servings: 10 - Prep: 20m - Cooks: 25m - Total: 50m

NUTRITION FACTS

Calories: 119, Carbohydrates: 13.6g, Fat: 1g, Protein: 13.2g, Cholesterol: 47mg

INGREDIENTS

- 2 cups coarsely chopped zucchini
- 1 egg
- 1 1/2 cups coarsely chopped onions
- 2 tablespoons Worcestershire sauce
- 1 red bell pepper, coarsely chopped
- 1 tablespoon Dijon mustard
- 1 pound extra lean ground turkey
- 1/2 cup barbecue sauce, or as needed
- 1/2 cup uncooked couscous

DIRECTIONS

1. Preheat oven to 400 degrees F (200 degrees C). Spray 20 muffin cups with cooking spray.

2. Place zucchini, onions, and red bell pepper into a food processor, and pulse several times until finely chopped but not liquefied. Place the vegetables into a bowl, and mix in ground turkey, couscous, egg, Worcestershire sauce, and Dijon mustard until thoroughly combined. Fill each prepared muffin cup about 3/4 full. Top each cup with about 1 teaspoon of barbecue sauce.

3. Bake in the preheated oven until juices run clear, about 25 minutes. Internal temperature of a muffin measured by an instant-read meat thermometer should be at least 160 degrees F (70 degrees C). Let stand 5 minutes before serving.

EASY BEEF STROGANOFF

Servings: 8 - Prep: 10m - Cooks: 20m - Total: 30m

NUTRITION FACTS

Calories: 602, Carbohydrates: 36.1g, Fat: 37.4g, Protein: 28.9g, Cholesterol: 148mg

INGREDIENTS

- 1 (12 ounce) package egg noodles, cooked and drained
- 4 tablespoons all-purpose flour
- 6 ounces fresh mushrooms, sliced
- 2 cups beef broth
- 1 onion, chopped
- 1 cup sour cream
- 1/4 cup butter
- salt and black pepper to taste
- 2 pounds lean ground beef

DIRECTIONS

1. Bring a large pot of water to a boil. Cook egg noodles in boiling water until done, about 8 minutes. Drain.

2. Meanwhile, prepare the sauce. In a large skillet, cook mushrooms and onions in 2 tablespoons of butter over medium heat until soft; remove from pan.

3. Using the same pan, melt remaining butter. Cook ground beef in melted butter until browned. Mix in flour. Stir in beef broth, and cook until slightly thickened. Add mushroom and onion mixture; stir in sour cream. Season to taste with salt and pepper. Continue cooking until sauce is hot, but not boiling. Serve sauce over egg noodles.

PORTOBELLO PENNE PASTA CASSEROLE

Servings: 8 - Prep: 15m - Cooks: 30m - Total: 45m

NUTRITION FACTS

Calories: 380, Carbohydrates: 32.1g, Fat: 21.3g, Protein: 16g, Cholesterol: 23mg

INGREDIENTS

- 1 (8 ounce) package uncooked penne pasta
- 1/2 teaspoon dried basil
- 2 tablespoons vegetable oil
- 2 cups milk
- 1/2 pound portobello mushrooms, thinly sliced
- 2 cups shredded mozzarella cheese
- 1/2 cup margarine
- 1 (10 ounce) package frozen chopped spinach, thawed
- 1/4 cup all-purpose flour
- 1/4 cup soy sauce
- 1 large clove garlic, minced

DIRECTIONS

1. Preheat oven to 350 degrees F (175 degrees C). Lightly grease a 9x13 inch baking dish.

2. Bring a large pot of lightly salted water to a boil. Place pasta in the pot, cook for 8 to 10 minutes, until al dente, and drain.

3. Heat the oil in a saucepan over medium heat. Stir in the mushrooms, cook 1 minute, and set aside. Melt margarine in the saucepan. Mix in flour, garlic, and basil. Gradually mix in milk until thickened. Stir in 1 cup cheese until melted. Remove saucepan from heat, and mix in cooked pasta, mushrooms, spinach, and soy sauce. Transfer to the prepared baking dish, and top with remaining cheese.

4. Bake 20 minutes in the preheated oven, until bubbly and lightly brown.

HEARTY VEGETABLE LASAGNA

Servings: 12 - Prep: 25m - Cooks: 1h - Total: 1h40m - Additional: 15m

NUTRITION FACTS

Calories: 462, Carbohydrates: 49.6g, Fat: 19.5g, Protein: 23.2g, Cholesterol: 77mg

INGREDIENTS

- 1 (16 ounce) package lasagna noodles
- 2 (26 ounce) jars pasta sauce
- 1 pound fresh mushrooms, sliced
- 1 teaspoon dried basil
- 3/4 cup chopped green bell pepper
- 1 (15 ounce) container part-skim ricotta cheese
- 3/4 cup chopped onion
- 4 cups shredded mozzarella cheese
- 3 cloves garlic, minced
- 2 eggs
- 2 tablespoons vegetable oil
- 1/2 cup grated Parmesan cheese

DIRECTIONS

1. Cook the lasagna noodles in a large pot of boiling water for 10 minutes, or until al dente. Rinse with cold water, and drain.
2. In a large saucepan, cook and stir mushrooms, green peppers, onion, and garlic in oil. Stir in pasta sauce and basil; bring to a boil. Reduce heat, and simmer 15 minutes.
3. Mix together ricotta, 2 cups mozzarella cheese, and eggs.
4. Preheat oven to 350 degrees F (175 degrees C). Spread 1 cup tomato sauce into the bottom of a greased 9x13 inch baking dish. Layer 1/2 each, lasagna noodles, ricotta mix, sauce, and Parmesan cheese. Repeat layering, and top with remaining 2 cups mozzarella cheese.
5. Bake, uncovered, for 40 minutes. Let stand 15 minutes before serving.

ITALIAN WEDDING SOUP

Servings: 4 - Prep: 20m - Cooks: 30m - Total: 50m

NUTRITION FACTS

Calories: 416, Carbohydrates: 43.3g, Fat: 14.2g, Protein: 27.3g, Cholesterol: 87mg

INGREDIENTS

- 1/2 pound extra-lean ground beef
- 1/2 teaspoon onion powder
- 1 egg, lightly beaten
- 5 3/4 cups chicken broth
- 2 tablespoons dry bread crumbs
- 2 cups thinly sliced escarole
- 1 tablespoon grated Parmesan cheese
- 1 cup uncooked orzo pasta
- 1/2 teaspoon dried basil
- 1/3 cup finely chopped carrot

DIRECTIONS

1. In medium bowl, combine meat, egg, bread crumbs, cheese, basil and onion powder; shape into 3/4 inch balls.

2. In large saucepan, heat broth to boiling; stir in escarole, orzo pasta, chopped carrot and meatballs. Return to boil, then reduce heat to medium. Cook at slow boil for 10 minutes, or until pasta is al dente. Stir frequently to prevent sticking.

BAKED ZITI WITH SAUSAGE

Servings: 8 - Prep: 30m - Cooks: 30m - Total: 1h

NUTRITION FACTS

Calories: 649, Carbohydrates: 68.9g, Fat: 27.4g, Protein: 30.7g, Cholesterol: 86mg

INGREDIENTS

- 1 (16 ounce) package dry ziti pasta
- 1 teaspoon dried oregano
- 1 pound mild Italian sausage
- 1/2 teaspoon salt
- 1 (15 ounce) container ricotta cheese
- 1/2 teaspoon ground black pepper
- 1 egg
- 1 1/2 (26 ounce) jars spaghetti sauce, divided
- 1 large yellow onion, minced
- 1 (8 ounce) package shredded Italian cheese blend
- 2 teaspoons minced garlic

- 1 teaspoon dried basil (optional)

DIRECTIONS

1. Preheat an oven to 350 degrees F (175 degrees C). Grease a 9x13 inch baking dish.

2. Fill a large pot with lightly salted water and bring to a rolling boil over high heat. Once the water is boiling, stir in the ziti, and return to a boil. Cook the pasta uncovered, stirring occasionally, until the pasta has cooked through, but is still firm to the bite, about 8 minutes. Drain well in a colander set in the sink.

3. While pasta is cooking, heat a large skillet over medium heat. Add the sausage, and cook and stir until brown, about 10 minutes. Drain sausage and set aside.

4. Stir together the ricotta, egg, onion, garlic, and oregano in a large bowl until well combined. Stir in the drained pasta, the drained sausage, salt, pepper, and 1/2 jar of the spaghetti sauce; mix well.

5. In the prepared baking dish, cover the bottom with 1/3 jar of spaghetti sauce. Layer 1/2 of the pasta mixture, 1/3 jar of spaghetti sauce, and 1/2 of the shredded cheese. Then layer the remaining 1/2 of the pasta, 1/3 of the sauce, and 1/2 of the cheese. Sprinkle with basil. Cover the dish tightly with aluminum foil.

6. Bake in the preheated oven until heated through, about 20 minutes. Uncover; return to the oven and bake until cheese is melted, 5 to 10 more minutes.

MANICOTTI ALLA ROMANA

Servings: 7 - Prep: 1h - Cooks: 50m - Total: 1h50m

NUTRITION FACTS

Calories: 612, Carbohydrates: 58.7g, Fat: 30.3g, Protein: 27.6g, Cholesterol: 134mg

INGREDIENTS

- 2 tablespoons olive oil
- 2 eggs, beaten
- 1/2 cup chopped onion
- 3 cups spaghetti sauce, divided
- 6 cloves garlic, finely chopped
- 2 tablespoons butter
- 1 pound ground beef
- 2 tablespoons all-purpose flour
- salt to taste
- 2 tablespoons chicken bouillon granules
- 1 (10 ounce) package frozen chopped spinach, thawed and drained

- 2 cups half-and-half
- 1 (12 ounce) package manicotti shells
- 1/4 cup chopped fresh parsley
- 2 cups ricotta cheese
- 1 tablespoon chopped fresh basil
- 1/2 cup grated Parmesan cheese

DIRECTIONS

1. Heat oil in a large skillet over medium heat. Saute onions until translucent. Saute garlic for 1 minute and stir in ground beef. Cook until well browned and crumbled. Season with salt and set aside to cool.

2. Cook spinach according to package directions. Meanwhile, bring a large pot of lightly salted water to a boil. Add manicotti shells and parboil for half of the time recommended on the package. Drain and cover with cool water to stop the cooking process and prevent the shells from cracking.

3. To the ground beef mixture add the cooked spinach and ricotta cheese. When the mixture is cool, add the beaten eggs. Spread 1/4 cup spaghetti sauce in the bottom of a 9x13 inch baking dish. Gently drain the manicotti shells and carefully stuff each one with the meat and cheese mixture; place shells in prepared dish. Lightly cover the dish with plastic wrap or a clean, damp towel to prevent shells from cracking.

4. Preheat oven to 350 degrees F (175 degrees C).

5. Prepare the white sauce by melting the butter in a small saucepan over medium heat. Stir in flour and chicken bouillon. Increase heat to medium-high and cook, stirring constantly, until it begins to bubble. Stir in half and half and bring to a boil, stirring frequently. Cook for 1 minute, stirring constantly. Remove from heat and stir in parsley. Pour or ladle the sauce evenly over the stuffed shells.

6. Stir the basil into the remaining spaghetti sauce. Carefully pour or ladle spaghetti sauce over the white sauce, trying to layer the sauces without mixing.

7. Cover and bake for 40 minutes. Remove from oven, uncover and sprinkle with Parmesan cheese. Bake, uncovered, for 10 minutes more.

GARLIC SHRIMP LINGUINE

Servings: 8 - Prep: 10m - Cooks: 20m - Total: 30m

NUTRITION FACTS

Calories: 287, Carbohydrates: 42.3g, Fat: 4.9g, Protein: 17.6g, Cholesterol: 77mg

INGREDIENTS

- 1 pound uncooked linguine
- 3 cloves garlic, minced

- 1 tablespoon butter

- 1 teaspoon chopped fresh parsley

- 3 tablespoons white wine

- 1 pinch salt and pepper to taste

- 2 teaspoons grated Parmesan cheese

- 1 pound medium shrimp, peeled and deveined

DIRECTIONS

1. Bring a large pot of lightly salted water to a boil. Add pasta and cook for 8 to 10 minutes or until al dente; drain.

2. In a medium saucepan, melt butter over medium low heat; add wine, cheese, garlic, parsley and salt and pepper to taste. Simmer over low heat for 3 to 5 minutes, stirring frequently.

3. Increase heat to medium high and add shrimp to saucepan; cook for about 3 to 4 minutes or until shrimp begins to turn pink. Do not overcook.

4. Divide pasta into portions and spoon sauce on top; garnish with Parmesan cheese and fresh parsley, if desired.

EGG NOODLES

Servings: 7 - Prep: 15m - Cooks: 3m - Total: 33m

NUTRITION FACTS

Calories: 206, Carbohydrates: 35g, Fat: 3.8g, Protein: 7g, Cholesterol: 59mg

INGREDIENTS

- 2 1/2 cups all-purpose flour

- 1/2 cup milk

- 1 pinch salt

- 1 tablespoon butter

- 2 eggs, beaten

DIRECTIONS

1. In a large bowl, stir together the flour and salt. Add the beaten egg, milk, and butter. Knead dough until smooth, about 5 minutes. Let rest in a covered bowl for 10 minutes.

2. On a floured surface, roll out to 1/8 or 1/4 inch thickness. Cut into desired lengths and shapes.

3. Allow to air dry before cooking.

4. To cook fresh pasta, in a large pot with boiling salted water cook until al dente.

BOB'S AWESOME LASAGNA

Servings: 12 - Prep: 30m - Cooks: 1h - Total: 1h30m

NUTRITION FACTS

Calories: 335, Carbohydrates: 26.2g, Fat: 14.6g, Protein: 24g, Cholesterol: 54mg

INGREDIENTS

- 8 ounces lasagna noodles
- 1/2 teaspoon garlic salt
- 1 pound ground beef
- 1 (32 ounce) jar spaghetti sauce
- 1/4 cup minced onions
- 1 (16 ounce) package large curd cottage cheese
- 1 teaspoon salt
- 1 pound mozzarella cheese, shredded

DIRECTIONS

1. Bring a large pot of lightly salted water to a boil. Cook noodles in boiling water for 8 to 10 minutes, or until al dente; drain.

2. In a large skillet over medium heat, saute ground beef, onions, salt and garlic salt until meat is brown. Drain excess fat, add spaghetti sauce to beef mixture, and bring to a boil. Reduce heat, and simmer for 15 to 20 minutes.

3. Preheat oven to 350 degrees F (175 degrees C). Grease a 9x13 inch glass baking pan.

4. Line bottom of pan with three lasagna noodles. Spread 1/3 of sauce mixture over noodles. Layer 1/3 of the cottage cheese over the sauce. Sprinkle 1/3 of the mozzarella over the cottage cheese. Repeat this layering process until all ingredients are used up.

5. Bake in the preheated oven for one hour. Let stand for 10 minutes before serving.

BEEFY BAKED RAVIOLI

Servings: 6 - Prep: 20m - Cooks: 30m - Total: 50m

NUTRITION FACTS

Calories: 465, Carbohydrates: 30.6g, Fat: 23.8g, Protein: 30.5g, Cholesterol: 100mg

INGREDIENTS

- 1 pound ground beef
- 1 cup shredded mozzarella cheese
- ½ (25 ounce) package frozen cheese ravioli

- 1 cup shredded Monterey Jack cheese

- 1 (14 ounce) jar spaghetti sauce

- 1 tablespoon grated Parmesan cheese

- 1 (14.5 ounce) can diced tomatoes, drained

DIRECTIONS

1. Preheat the oven to 450 degrees F (230 degrees C).

2. Crumble the ground beef into a large skillet over medium-high heat. Cook and stir until no longer pink. Drain grease, then stir in the spaghetti sauce and tomatoes.

3. Spread 1/3 of the sauce in the bottom of an 11x7 inch baking dish. Arrange 1/2 of the ravioli over the sauce. Sprinkle 1/2 of the mozzarella cheese and 1/2 of the Monterey Jack cheese over the ravioli. Repeat layers, ending with the last of the sauce on top. Cover with aluminum foil.

4. Bake for 30 minutes in the preheated oven. Sprinkle Parmesan cheese over the top before serving.

SIMPLE BEEF STROGANOFF

Servings: 4 - Prep: 20m - Cooks: 10m - Total: 30m

NUTRITION FACTS

Calories: 679, Carbohydrates: 48.2g, Fat: 40.5g, Protein: 28.7g, Cholesterol: 159mg

INGREDIENTS

- 1 (8 ounce) package egg noodles

- 1 tablespoon garlic powder

- 1 pound ground beef

- 1/2 cup sour cream

- 1 (10.75 ounce) can fat free condensed cream of mushroom soup

- salt and pepper to taste

DIRECTIONS

1. Prepare the egg noodles according to package directions and set aside.

2. In a separate large skillet over medium heat, saute the ground beef over medium heat for 5 to 10 minutes, or until browned. Drain the fat and add the soup and garlic powder. Simmer for 10 minutes, stirring occasionally.

3. Remove from heat and combine the meat mixture with the egg noodles. Add the sour cream, stirring well, and season with salt and pepper to taste.

PENNE WITH CHICKEN AND PESTO

Servings: 8 - Prep: 20m - Cooks: 10m - Total: 30m

NUTRITION FACTS

Calories: 497, Carbohydrates: 42.6g, Fat: 26.1g, Protein: 24g, Cholesterol: 97mg

INGREDIENTS

- 1 (16 ounce) package penne pasta
- salt and pepper to taste
- 2 tablespoons butter
- 1 1/4 cups heavy cream
- 2 tablespoons olive oil
- 1/4 cup pesto
- 4 skinless, boneless chicken breast halves - cut into thin strips
- 3 tablespoons grated Parmesan cheese
- 2 cloves garlic, minced

DIRECTIONS

1. Bring a large pot of lightly salted water to a boil. Add pasta and cook for 8 to 10 minutes or until al dente; drain.

2. Heat butter and olive oil in a large skillet over medium heat. Saute chicken and garlic until chicken is almost cooked. Reduce heat and stir in salt, pepper, cream, pesto and Parmesan cheese. Cook until chicken is no longer pink inside. Stir in cooked pasta.

BEEF STROGANOFF FOR INSTANT POT

Servings: 8 - Prep: 20m - Cooks: 37m - Total: 1h2m - Additional: 5m

NUTRITION FACTS

Calories: 536, Carbohydrates: 45.2g, Fat: 26.2g, Protein: 29g, Cholesterol: 121mg

INGREDIENTS

- 2 tablespoons canola oil
- 2 tablespoons soy sauce
- 1/2 onion, diced
- 3 cups chopped mushrooms
- 2 teaspoons salt, divided
- 2 tablespoons all-purpose flour
- 2 pounds beef stew meat, cut into 1-inch cubes
- 3 cups chicken broth
- 1 teaspoon freshly ground black pepper
- 1 (16 ounce) package wide egg noodles

- 3 cloves garlic, minced
- 3/4 cup sour cream, or to taste
- 1/2 teaspoon dried thyme

DIRECTIONS

1. Turn on a multi-cooker (such as Instant Pot®) and select Saute function. Heat oil for 1 minute. Add onion and 1/2 teaspoon salt; cook and stir until onion begins to soften, 3 to 4 minutes.

2. Season beef with 1 teaspoon salt and pepper. Add to the pot. Cook and stir until browned evenly on all sides, about 2 minutes. Add garlic and thyme; cook until fragrant, about 30 seconds. Pour in soy sauce.

3. Stir mushrooms into the pot. Stir in flour until evenly incorporated. Pour in chicken broth and remaining 1/2 teaspoon salt. Close and lock the lid. Set timer for 10 minutes. Set to high pressure according to manufacturer's instructions, 10 to 15 minutes.

4. Release pressure carefully using the quick-release method. Open pressure cooker; stir in egg noodles. Seal and bring to high pressure again, about 5 minutes; cook for 5 minutes.

5. Release pressure naturally according to manufacturer's instruction for 5 minutes. Release remaining pressure using the quick-release method. Open pressure cooker; stir in sour cream.

SPINACH AND ORZO SALAD

Servings: 8 - Prep: 20m - Cooks: 1h - Total: 1h20m - Additional: 1h

NUTRITION FACTS

Calories: 490, Carbohydrates: 49g, Fat: 26.9g, Protein: 15.8g, Cholesterol: 25mg

INGREDIENTS

- 1 (16 ounce) package uncooked orzo pasta
- 1/2 teaspoon dried basil
- 1 (10 ounce) package baby spinach leaves, finely chopped
- 1/4 teaspoon ground white pepper
- 1/2 pound crumbled feta cheese
- 1/2 cup olive oil
- 1/2 red onion, finely chopped
- 1/2 cup balsamic vinegar
- 3/4 cup pine nuts

DIRECTIONS

1. Bring a large pot of lightly salted water to a boil. Add orzo and cook for 8 to 10 minutes or until al dente; drain and rinse with cold water. Transfer to a large bowl and stir in spinach, feta, onion, pine nuts, basil and white pepper. Toss with olive oil and balsamic vinegar. Refrigerate and serve cold.

JENN'S OUT OF THIS WORLD SPAGHETTI AND MEATBALLS

Servings: 8 - Prep: 15m - Cooks: 1h - Total: 1h15m

NUTRITION FACTS

Calories: 572, Carbohydrates: 80.1g, Fat: 17g, Protein: 27.7g, Cholesterol: 87mg

INGREDIENTS

- 3 tablespoons olive oil
- 1 dried bay leaf
- 3/4 cup chopped onion
- salt and pepper to taste
- 4 cloves garlic, minced
- 1 pound ground round
- 2 (16 ounce) cans crushed tomatoes
- 1/2 cup Italian seasoned bread crumbs
- 3 (6 ounce) cans tomato paste
- 1/4 cup chopped fresh parsley
- 1 cup water
- 2 eggs, lightly beaten
- 1/2 cup sugar
- 1/2 cup grated Parmesan cheese
- 1/4 cup chopped fresh oregano, divided
- 1 (16 ounce) package uncooked spaghetti

DIRECTIONS

1. Heat the olive oil in a large saucepan over medium heat, and cook the onion until lightly brown. Mix in 2 cloves garlic, and cook 1 minute. Stir in crushed tomatoes, tomato paste, water, sugar, 1/2 the oregano, and bay leaf. Season with salt and pepper. Bring to a boil, reduce heat to low, and simmer while preparing meatballs.

2. In a bowl, mix the ground round, bread crumbs, remaining oregano, remaining garlic, parsley, eggs, and cheese. Season with salt and pepper. Roll into 1 inch balls, and drop into the sauce. Cook 40 minutes in the sauce, or until internal temperature of meatballs reaches a minimum of 160 degrees F (72 degrees C).

3. Bring a large pot of lightly salted water to a boil, and stir in the spaghetti. Cook 8 to 10 minutes, until al dente, and drain. Serve the meatballs and sauce over the cooked spaghetti.

CHICKEN TETRAZZINI

Servings: 4 - Prep: 15m - Cooks: 45m - Total: 1h

NUTRITION FACTS

Calories: 730, Carbohydrates: 52.7g, Fat: 42.6g, Protein: 33.1g, Cholesterol: 173mg

INGREDIENTS

- 1 (8 ounce) package spaghetti, broken into pieces
- 1 cup heavy cream
- 1/4 cup butter
- 2 tablespoons sherry
- 1/4 cup all-purpose flour
- 1 (4.5 ounce) can sliced mushrooms, drained
- 3/4 teaspoon salt
- 2 cups chopped cooked chicken
- 1/4 teaspoon ground black pepper
- 1/2 cup grated Parmesan cheese
- 1 cup chicken broth

DIRECTIONS

1. Preheat oven to 350 degrees F (175 degrees C). Lightly grease a 9x13 inch baking dish.

2. Bring a large pot of lightly salted water to a boil. Add spaghetti, and cook for 8 to 10 minutes, or until al dente; drain.

3. Meanwhile, in a large saucepan, melt butter over low heat. Stir in flour, salt, and pepper. Cook, stirring, until smooth. Remove from heat, and gradually stir in chicken broth and cream.

4. Return to heat, and bring to a low boil for 1 minute, stirring constantly. Add sherry, then stir in cooked spaghetti, mushrooms, and chicken. Pour mixture into the prepared baking dish, and top with Parmesan cheese.

5. Bake 30 minutes in the preheated oven, until bubbly and lightly browned.

PASTA PRIMAVERA WITH ITALIAN TURKEY SAUSAGE

Servings: 8 - Prep: 20m - Cooks: 20m - Total: 50m

NUTRITION FACTS

Calories: 477, Carbohydrates: 50.1g, Fat: 21.8g, Protein: 20.5g, Cholesterol: 38mg

INGREDIENTS

- 1 (16 ounce) package uncooked farfalle pasta
- 6 roma (plum) tomatoes, chopped
- 1 pound hot Italian turkey sausage, cut into 1/2 inch slices
- 1 green bell pepper, chopped
- 1/2 cup olive oil, divided
- 20 leaves fresh basil
- 4 cloves garlic, diced
- 2 teaspoons chicken bouillon granules
- 1/2 onion, diced
- 1/2 teaspoon red pepper flakes
- 2 small zucchini, chopped
- 1/2 cup grated Parmesan cheese
- 2 small yellow squash, chopped

DIRECTIONS

1. Bring a large pot of lightly salted water to a boil. Place farfalle in pot and cook 8 to 10 minutes, until al dente; drain.

2. Place sausage in a large skillet over medium heat and cook until evenly brown; set aside. Heat 1/4 cup oil in skillet. Stir in garlic and onion, and cook until tender. Mix in zucchini, squash, tomatoes, bell pepper and basil. Dissolve bouillon in the mixture. Season with red pepper. Stir in remaining oil. Continue cooking 10 minutes.

3. Mix pasta, sausage and cheese into skillet. Continue cooking 5 minutes, or until heated through.

OLD FASHIONED MAC AND CHEESE

Servings: 7 - Prep: 20m - Cooks: 45m - Total: 1h5m

NUTRITION FACTS

Calories: , Carbohydrates: g, Fat: g, Protein: g, Cholesterol: mg

INGREDIENTS

- 2 cups uncooked elbow macaroni
- salt and pepper to taste
- 4 tablespoons butter
- 1/4 pound processed cheese food

- 2 tablespoons all-purpose flour
- 1/4 pound shredded Cheddar cheese
- 2 cups milk
- 1/4 pound shredded Swiss cheese
- 1/4 onion, minced

DIRECTIONS

1. Preheat oven to 350 degrees F (175 degrees C).
2. Prepare the elbow macaroni according to package directions.
3. Meanwhile, melt the butter in a small saucepan over medium high heat. Stir in the flour until a cream colored paste forms. Then pour in the milk and stir constantly until this comes to a hard boil, then stir for 1 more minute. Remove from heat and set aside.
4. When the macaroni is cooked, spread 1/2 of it into the bottom of a lightly greased 9x13-inch baking dish. Then layer 1/2 of the grated onion, 1/2 of the salt and pepper and 1/2 of each of the cheeses. Repeat this one more time: macaroni, onion, salt and pepper and cheeses, and then pour the reserved white sauce over all. Top off with small pats of butter to taste.
5. Cover and bake at 350 degrees F (175 degrees C) for 45 minutes.

MAMA'S ITALIAN WEDDING SOUP

Servings: 10 - Prep: 20m - Cooks: 25m - Total: 45m

NUTRITION FACTS

Calories: 169, Carbohydrates: 12.7g, Fat: 6.9g, Protein: 13.11g, Cholesterol: 71mg

INGREDIENTS

- 1 pound extra-lean ground beef
- 3 tablespoons minced onion
- 2 eggs, beaten
- 2 1/2 quarts chicken broth
- 1/4 cup dried bread crumbs
- 2 cups spinach - packed, rinsed and thinly sliced
- 2 tablespoons grated Parmesan cheese
- 1 cup seashell pasta
- 1 teaspoon dried basil
- 3/4 cup diced carrots

DIRECTIONS

1. In a medium bowl, combine the beef, egg, bread crumbs, cheese, basil and onion. Shape mixture into 3/4-inch balls and set aside.

2. In a large stockpot heat chicken broth to boiling; stir in the spinach, pasta, carrot and meatballs. Return to boil; reduce heat to medium. Cook, stirring frequently, at a slow boil for 10 minutes or until pasta is al dente, and meatballs are no longer pink inside. Serve hot with Parmesan cheese sprinkled on top.

CREAMY CHICKEN LASAGNA

Servings: 6 - Prep: 25m - Cooks: 1h5m - Total: 1h30m

NUTRITION FACTS

Calories: 495, Carbohydrates: 36.2g, Fat: 26.4g, Protein: 28g, Cholesterol: 104mg

INGREDIENTS

- 3 skinless, boneless chicken breast halves
- 1 (8 ounce) package cream cheese, softened
- 6 uncooked lasagna noodles
- 2 cups shredded mozzarella cheese
- 1 cube chicken bouillon
- 1 (26 ounce) jar spaghetti sauce
- 1/4 cup hot water

DIRECTIONS

1. Bring a large pot of lightly salted water to a boil. Cook lasagna noodles for 8 to 10 minutes, or until al dente. Drain, rinse with cold water, and set aside.

2. Meanwhile, place the chicken in a saucepan with enough water to cover, and bring to a boil. Cook for 20 minutes, or until no longer pink and juices run clear. Remove from saucepan, and shred.

3. Preheat oven to 350 degrees F (175 degrees C). Dissolve the bouillon cube in hot water. In a large bowl, mix the chicken with the bouillon, cream cheese, and 1 cup mozzarella cheese.

4. Spread 1/3 of spaghetti sauce in the bottom of a 9x13 inch baking dish. Cover with the chicken mixture, and top with 3 lasagna noodles; repeat. Top with remaining sauce, and sprinkle with remaining mozzarella cheese.

5. Bake for 45 minutes in the preheated oven.

SESAME NOODLES

Servings: 8 - Prep: 15m - Cooks: 15m - Total: 30m

NUTRITION FACTS

Calories: 371, Carbohydrates: 52g, Fat: 14.8g, Protein: 7.9g, Cholesterol: 0mg

INGREDIENTS

- 1 (16 ounce) package linguine pasta

- 6 tablespoons soy sauce

- 6 cloves garlic, minced

- 2 tablespoons sesame oil

- 6 tablespoons sugar

- 2 teaspoons chili sauce

- 6 tablespoons safflower oil

- 6 green onions, sliced

- 6 tablespoons rice vinegar

- 1 teaspoon sesame seeds, toasted

DIRECTIONS

1. Bring a pot of lightly salted water to boil. Add pasta, and cook until al dente, about 8 to 10 minutes. Drain, and transfer to a serving bowl.

2. Meanwhile, place a saucepan over medium-high heat. Stir in garlic, sugar, oil, vinegar, soy sauce, sesame oil, and chili sauce. Bring to a boil, stirring constantly, until sugar dissolves. Pour sauce over linguine, and toss to coat. Garnish with green onions and sesame seeds.

BAKED PENNE WITH ITALIAN SAUSAGE

Servings: 6 - Prep: 15m - Cooks: 35m - Total: 50m

NUTRITION FACTS

Calories: , Carbohydrates: g, Fat: g, Protein: g, Cholesterol: mg

INGREDIENTS

- 1 (12 ounce) package dry penne pasta

- 1 (15 ounce) can tomato sauce

- 2 teaspoons olive oil

- 1 (14.5 ounce) can diced tomatoes with garlic

- 1 pound mild Italian sausage

- 1 (6 ounce) can tomato paste

- 1 cup chopped onion

- 2 cups shredded mozzarella cheese

- 1/2 cup white wine

DIRECTIONS

1. Preheat oven to 350 degrees F (175 degrees C). Bring a large pot of lightly salted water to a boil. Add pasta and cook for 8 to 10 minutes or until al dente; drain.

2. Heat oil in a large, deep skillet. Place sausage and onion in the skillet and cook over medium high heat until evenly brown. Drain excess fat. Pour in wine, and cook for 1 minute, stirring, to deglaze the pan. Stir in tomato sauce, diced tomatoes and tomato paste. Simmer for 10 minutes, stirring occasionally. Toss with cooked pasta, and place in a 9x13 inch baking dish. Sprinkle top with mozzarella.

3. Bake in preheated oven for 20 minutes, or until cheese is melted.

GREEK PENNE AND CHICKEN

Servings: 4 - Prep: 20m - Cooks: 30m - Total: 50m

NUTRITION FACTS

Calories: 685, Carbohydrates: 96.2g, Fat: 13.2g, Protein: 47g, Cholesterol: 94mg

INGREDIENTS

- 1 (16 ounce) package penne pasta
- 1/2 cup crumbled feta cheese
- 1 1/2 tablespoons butter
- 3 tablespoons chopped fresh parsley
- 1/2 cup chopped red onion
- 2 tablespoons lemon juice
- 2 cloves garlic, minced
- 1 teaspoon dried oregano
- 1 pound skinless, boneless chicken breast halves - cut into bite-size pieces
- salt to taste
- 1 (14 ounce) can artichoke hearts in water
- ground black pepper to taste
- 1 tomato, chopped

DIRECTIONS

1. In a large pot with boiling salted water cook penne pasta until al dente. Drain.

2. Meanwhile, in a large skillet over medium-high heat melt butter, add onion and garlic and cook for 2 minutes. Add chopped chicken and continue cooking, stirring occasionally until golden brown, about 5 to 6 minutes.

3. Reduce heat to medium- low. Drain and chop artichoke hearts and add them, chopped tomato, feta cheese, fresh parsley, lemon juice, dried oregano, and drained penne pasta to the large skillet. Cook until heated through, about 2 to 3 minutes.

4. Season with salt and ground black pepper. Serve warm.

HOME STYLE MACARONI AND CHEESE

Servings: 6 - Prep: 20m - Cooks: 20m - Total: 40m

NUTRITION FACTS

Calories: 641, Carbohydrates: 47g, Fat: 40.4g, Protein: 22.6g, Cholesterol: 118mg

INGREDIENTS

- 7 ounces macaroni
- 1/2 teaspoon black pepper
- 1/4 cup butter
- 2 teaspoons Dijon mustard
- 3 tablespoons all-purpose flour
- 2 cups shredded Cheddar cheese
- 2 cups milk
- 1 cup dry bread crumbs
- 1 (8 ounce) package cream cheese
- 2 tablespoons butter
- 1/2 teaspoon salt
- 2 tablespoons chopped fresh parsley

DIRECTIONS

1. Preheat oven to 400 degrees F (200 degrees C).
2. Bring a large pot of lightly salted water to a boil. Add macaroni pasta and cook for 8 to 10 minutes or until al dente; drain.
3. In a 3 quart saucepan over medium heat, melt butter and stir in flour. Cook for about 1 minute, until smooth and bubbly; stirring occasionally. Mix in milk, cream cheese, salt, pepper, and Dijon mustard. Continue cooking until sauce is thickened. Add cooked macaroni and Cheddar cheese.
4. Pour into 2 quart casserole dish. In small bowl mix together bread crumbs, butter and parsley; spread over macaroni and cheese. Bake for 15 to 20 minutes or until golden brown and heated through.

PAD THAI

Servings: 6 - Prep: 40m - Cooks: 20m - Total: 1h

NUTRITION FACTS

Calories: 524, Carbohydrates: 58.5g, Fat: 20.7g, Protein: 26.4g, Cholesterol: 178mg

INGREDIENTS

- 1 (12 ounce) package rice noodles
- 3 tablespoons white sugar
- 2 tablespoons butter
- 1/8 tablespoon crushed red pepper
- 1 pound boneless, skinless chicken breast halves, cut into bite-sized pieces
- 2 cups bean sprouts
- 1/4 cup vegetable oil
- 1/4 cup crushed peanuts
- 4 eggs
- 3 green onions, chopped
- 1 tablespoon white wine vinegar
- 1 lemon, cut into wedges
- 2 tablespoons fish sauce

DIRECTIONS

1. Soak rice noodles in cold water 30 to 50 minutes, or until soft. Drain, and set aside.
2. Heat butter in a wok or large heavy skillet. Saute chicken until browned. Remove, and set aside. Heat oil in wok over medium-high heat. Crack eggs into hot oil, and cook until firm. Stir in chicken, and cook for 5 minutes. Add softened noodles, and vinegar, fish sauce, sugar and red pepper. Adjust seasonings to taste. Mix while cooking, until noodles are tender. Add bean sprouts, and mix for 3 minutes.

MANICOTTI

Servings: 4 - Prep: 30m - Cooks: 45m - Total: 1h15m

NUTRITION FACTS

Calories: 676, Carbohydrates: 53.2g, Fat: 30.9g, Protein: 46g, Cholesterol: 189mg

INGREDIENTS

- 1 pint part-skim ricotta cheese
- salt to taste
- 8 ounces shredded mozzarella cheese
- ground black pepper to taste
- 3/4 cup grated Parmesan cheese
- 1 (16 ounce) jar spaghetti sauce
- 2 eggs
- 5 1/2 ounces manicotti pasta
- 1 teaspoon dried parsley

DIRECTIONS

1. Cook manicotti in boiling water until done. Drain, and rinse with cold water.

2. Preheat oven to 350 degrees F (175 degrees C).

3. In a large bowl, combine ricotta, mozzarella, and 1/2 cup Parmesan, eggs, parsley, and salt and pepper. Mix well.

4. Pour 1/2 cup sauce into an 11x17 inch baking dish. Fill each manicotti shell with 3 tablespoons cheese mixture, and arrange over sauce . Pour remaining sauce over top, and sprinkle with remaining Parmesan cheese.

5. Bake 45 minutes, or until bubbly.

PENNE AND VODKA SAUCE

Servings: 4 - Prep: 10m - Cooks: 15m - Total: 25m

NUTRITION FACTS

Calories: 795, Carbohydrates: 87.9g, Fat: 35.2g, Protein: 23.9g, Cholesterol: 84mg

INGREDIENTS

- 1 (16 ounce) package penne pasta
- 1/2 cup heavy whipping cream
- 2 tablespoons butter
- 1 1/2 cups tomato sauce
- 1/4 pound thinly sliced pancetta bacon, chopped
- 1/2 cup grated Parmesan cheese
- 1/3 cup vodka

DIRECTIONS

1. Bring a large pot of lightly salted water to a boil. Add pasta and cook for 8 to 10 minutes or until al dente; drain.

2. Meanwhile, melt butter or margarine in a large skillet over medium heat. Add pancetta, and saute until lightly browned. Add vodka and stir until it is reduced by half, about 4 to 5 minutes. Stir in tomato sauce and cream. Simmer uncovered for 10 to 12 minutes. Stir every few minutes.

3. Stir in pasta, and heat through. Serve with Parmesan cheese.

VIETNAMESE FRESH SPRING ROLLS

Servings: 8 - Prep: 45m - Cooks: 5m - Total: 50m

NUTRITION FACTS

Calories: 82, Carbohydrates: 15.8g, Fat: 0.7g, Protein: 3.3g, Cholesterol: 11mg

INGREDIENTS

- 2 ounces rice vermicelli
- 1/4 cup water
- 8 rice wrappers (8.5 inch diameter)
- 2 tablespoons fresh lime juice
- 8 large cooked shrimp - peeled, deveined and cut in half
- 1 clove garlic, minced
- 1 1/3 tablespoons chopped fresh Thai basil
- 2 tablespoons white sugar
- 3 tablespoons chopped fresh mint leaves
- 1/2 teaspoon garlic chili sauce
- 3 tablespoons chopped fresh cilantro
- 3 tablespoons hoisin sauce
- 2 leaves lettuce, chopped
- 1 teaspoon finely chopped peanuts
- 4 teaspoons fish sauce

DIRECTIONS

1. Bring a medium saucepan of water to boil. Boil rice vermicelli 3 to 5 minutes, or until al dente, and drain.
2. Fill a large bowl with warm water. Dip one wrapper into the hot water for 1 second to soften. Lay wrapper flat. In a row across the center, place 2 shrimp halves, a handful of vermicelli, basil, mint, cilantro and lettuce, leaving about 2 inches uncovered on each side. Fold uncovered sides inward, then tightly roll the wrapper, beginning at the end with the lettuce. Repeat with remaining ingredients.
3. In a small bowl, mix the fish sauce, water, lime juice, garlic, sugar and chili sauce.
4. In another small bowl, mix the hoisin sauce and peanuts.
5. Serve rolled spring rolls with the fish sauce and hoisin sauce mixtures.

SIMPLE MACARONI AND CHEESE

Servings: 4 - Prep: 10m - Cooks: 20m - Total: 30m

NUTRITION FACTS

Calories: 630, Carbohydrates: 55g, Fat: 33.6g, Protein: 26.5g, Cholesterol: 100mg

INGREDIENTS

- 1 (8 ounce) box elbow macaroni
- ground black pepper to taste

- 1/4 cup butter
- 2 cups milk
- 1/4 cup all-purpose flour
- 2 cups shredded Cheddar cheese
- 1/2 teaspoon salt

DIRECTIONS

1. Bring a large pot of lightly salted water to a boil. Cook elbow macaroni in the boiling water, stirring occasionally until cooked through but firm to the bite, 8 minutes. Drain.
2. Melt butter in a saucepan over medium heat; stir in flour, salt, and pepper until smooth, about 5 minutes. Slowly pour milk into butter-flour mixture while continuously stirring until mixture is smooth and bubbling, about 5 minutes. Add Cheddar cheese to milk mixture and stir until cheese is melted, 2 to 4 minutes.
3. Fold macaroni into cheese sauce until coated.

MANICOTTI ITALIAN CASSEROLE

Servings: 8 - Prep: 10m - Cooks: 30m - Total: 40m

NUTRITION FACTS

Calories: 909, Carbohydrates: 77.6g, Fat: 43g, Protein: 52.1g, Cholesterol: 127mg

INGREDIENTS

- 1 pound rigatoni pasta
- 2 (32 ounce) jars spaghetti sauce
- 1 pound ground beef
- 1 1/2 pounds shredded mozzarella cheese
- 1 pound Italian sausage
- thinly sliced pepperoni
- 1 (8 ounce) can mushrooms, drained

DIRECTIONS

1. Preheat oven to 350 degrees F (175 degrees C).
2. Bring a large pot of lightly salted water to boil. Pour in rigatoni, and cook until al dente, about 8 to 10 minutes. Drain, and set pasta aside.
3. Meanwhile, brown ground beef and italian sausage in a large skillet over medium heat. With a slotted spoon, remove beef and sausage to a baking dish. Stir mushrooms, spaghetti sauce, and cooked pasta into the baking dish. Sprinkle cheese and pepperoni over the top.
4. Bake in preheated oven until the cheese is brown and bubbly, about 20 minutes.

FRA DIAVOLO SAUCE WITH PASTA

Servings: 8 - Prep: 20m - Cooks: 40m - Total: 1h

NUTRITION FACTS

Calories: 335, Carbohydrates: 46.3g, Fat: 8.9g, Protein: 18.7g, Cholesterol: 52mg

INGREDIENTS

- 4 tablespoons olive oil, divided
- 1 (16 ounce) package linguine pasta
- 6 cloves garlic, crushed
- 8 ounces small shrimp, peeled and deveined
- 3 cups whole peeled tomatoes with liquid, chopped
- 8 ounces bay scallops
- 1 1/2 teaspoons salt
- 1 tablespoon chopped fresh parsley
- 1 teaspoon crushed red pepper flakes

DIRECTIONS

1. In a large saucepan, heat 2 tablespoons of the olive oil with the garlic over medium heat. When the garlic starts to sizzle, pour in the tomatoes. Season with salt and red pepper. Bring to a boil. Lower the heat, and simmer for 30 minutes, stirring occasionally.

2. Meanwhile, bring a large pot of lightly salted water to a boil. Cook pasta for 8 to 10 minutes, or until al dente; drain.

3. In a large skillet, heat the remaining 2 tablespoons of olive oil over high heat. Add the shrimp and scallops. Cook for about 2 minutes, stirring frequently, or until the shrimp turn pink. Add shrimp and scallops to the tomato mixture, and stir in the parsley. Cook for 3 to 4 minutes, or until the sauce just begins to bubble. Serve sauce over pasta.

HIYASHI CHUKA NOODLES

Servings: 2 - Prep: 15m - Cooks: 5m - Total: 20m

NUTRITION FACTS

Calories: 236, Carbohydrates: 28.5g, Fat: 10g, Protein: 9.3g, Cholesterol: 101mg

INGREDIENTS

- 3 tablespoons soy sauce
- 1 egg, beaten
- 2 tablespoons white sugar

- 1/2 cucumber, julienned

- 3 tablespoons white vinegar

- 1 carrot, grated

- 5 tablespoons chicken stock

- 1 slice cooked ham, cut into thin strips

- 1 teaspoon sesame oil

- 1/4 sheet nori, cut into thin slices

- 1/2 teaspoon chili oil (optional)

- 1 tablespoon hot Chinese mustard (optional)

- 2 (3 ounce) packages ramen noodles

DIRECTIONS

1. Mix the soy sauce, sugar, vinegar, chicken stock, sesame oil, and chili oil together in a small bowl, and stir until the sugar dissolves. Set aside.

2. Bring a saucepan of water to a boil. Add the ramen noodles and cook for 2 minutes. Drain immediately, and refrigerate noodles until cold. Meanwhile, heat a small nonstick skillet over medium heat. Pour in the beaten egg and tilt the pan to thinly coat the bottom with egg. When firm, fold the egg in half and remove from the pan. Slice into thin strips.

3. To serve, place cold noodles on serving plates. Top with separate piles of egg, cucumber, carrot, and ham. Pour the sauce over the top and sprinkle with crumbled nori. Serve with a touch of hot mustard on the side.

RIGATONI ALLA GENOVESE

Servings: 8 - Prep: 30m - Cooks: 9h30m - Total: 10h

NUTRITION FACTS

Calories: 891, Carbohydrates: 116.8g, Fat: 29.5g, Protein: 38.9g, Cholesterol: 80mg

INGREDIENTS

- 1 tablespoon olive oil

- 1 bay leaf

- 6 ounces pancetta or salt pork, diced

- 2/3 cup white wine

- 2 1/2 pounds beef chuck

- 4 pounds yellow onions, sliced

- 2 teaspoons kosher salt

- 2 pounds red onions, sliced

- 1/2 cup diced celery
- salt to taste
- 1/2 cup diced carrot
- 2 (16 ounce) boxes uncooked rigatoni
- 1 teaspoon kosher salt
- 1 tablespoon chopped fresh marjoram leaves
- 1 teaspoon freshly ground black pepper
- 1 pinch cayenne pepper
- 1 tablespoon tomato paste
- 2 tablespoons freshly grated Parmigiano-Reggiano cheese

DIRECTIONS

1. Heat oil in a large pot over medium heat. Cook pancetta until most of fat is rendered out, about 6 minutes. Remove cooked pancetta with a slotted spoon and save.

2. Raise heat to high and transfer meat to the pot. Season with salt. Cook and stir until liquid releases from beef and begins to evaporate, and meat browns, 10 to 15 minutes.

3. Reduce heat to medium-high. Add celery, carrots, reserved cooked pancetta, salt and pepper. Cook and stir about 5 minutes. Add a heaping tablespoon of tomato paste, bay leaf, and white wine. Cook and stir, scraping up the brownings from the bottom of the pan, 2 to 3 minutes. Add sliced onions. Reduce heat to medium. Cover pot and cook 30 minutes without stirring. After 30 minutes, stir onions and meat until well mixed. Cover again, and cook another 30 minutes. Stir.

4. Reduce heat to low and cook uncovered 8 to 10 hours, stirring occasionally. Skim off fat as mixture cooks. If sauce seems to reduce too much, add water or broth as needed to maintain a sauce-like consistency. Cook until beef and onions seem to melt into each other.

5. Bring a large pot of lightly salted water to a boil. Cook rigatoni in the boiling water, stirring occasionally until just barely al dente, 10 to 12 minutes. Drain.

6. Add rigatoni to the sauce and cook until heated through. Serve topped with a pinch of marjoram and freshly grated Parmigiano-Reggiano cheese.

BUFFALO CHICKEN STUFFED SHELLS

Servings: 6 - Prep: 15m - Cooks: 25m - Total: 3h40m - Additional: 3h

NUTRITION FACTS

Calories: 698, Carbohydrates: 62.8g, Fat: 29g, Protein: 44.4g, Cholesterol: 126mg

INGREDIENTS

- 1 pound ground chicken

- cooking spray
- ¼ cup butter
- 1 (16 ounce) package jumbo pasta shells
- 1 cup cayenne pepper sauce (such as Frank's RedHot)
- 1 (8 ounce) package shredded Cheddar-Monterey Jack cheese blend
- 1 (16 ounce) container whipped ricotta cheese
- salt and ground black pepper to taste

DIRECTIONS

1. Heat a large skillet over medium-high heat. Cook and stir ground chicken in the hot skillet until browned and crumbly, 5 to 7 minutes; drain and discard grease.
2. Melt butter in the skillet with the cooked chicken. Stir cayenne pepper sauce into the chicken mixture and remove from heat.
3. Squeeze as much moisture from the ricotta cheese using a cheese cloth or paper towels; put drained cheese in a large bowl. Add chicken mixture to the cheese and stir. Refrigerate until completely chilled, 3 to 4 hours.
4. Preheat oven to 375 degrees F (190 degrees C). Prepare a 13x9-inch baking dish with cooking spray.
5. Bring a large pot of lightly salted water to a boil. Cook pasta shells in the boiling water until cooked through but firm to the bite, about 10 minutes; drain. Rinse with cold water until no longer hot; drain.
6. Spoon chicken mixture into cooked pasta shells and arrange into the prepared baking dish. Sprinkle Cheddar-Monterey Jack cheese blend over the stuffed shells; season with salt and pepper.
7. Bake in preheated oven until the cheese is slightly melted and the stuffing is hot in the middle, 15 to 20 minutes.

'GOT SOME CRUST' MACARONI AND CHEESE

Servings: 12 - Prep: 20m - Cooks: 55m - Total: 1h15m

NUTRITION FACTS

Calories: 286, Carbohydrates: 23.2g, Fat: 15.5g, Protein: 13.1g, Cholesterol: 45mg

INGREDIENTS

- 2 cups elbow macaroni
- 1/4 teaspoon hot pepper sauce (such as Tabasco)
- 1/4 cup butter, divided
- 1 teaspoon prepared yellow mustard

- 1 small onion, chopped

- 2 cups shredded Cheddar cheese

- 2 tablespoons all-purpose flour

- 1/4 cup grated Parmesan cheese

- 1 1/2 cups milk

- 1 cup shredded Cheddar cheese

- 1 teaspoon salt

- 1/4 cup grated Parmesan cheese

- 1 teaspoon white pepper

- 1 cup dry bread crumbs

- 1 teaspoon Worcestershire sauce

DIRECTIONS

1. Preheat an oven to 350 degrees F (175 degrees C). Grease a 9x13 inch glass baking dish.

2. Fill a large pot with lightly salted water and bring to a rolling boil over high heat. Once the water is boiling, stir in the macaroni, and return to a boil. Cook the pasta uncovered, stirring occasionally, until the pasta has cooked through, but is still firm to the bite, about 8 minutes. Drain and mix with half of the butter.

3. While the macaroni is boiling, melt the remaining butter in a saucepan over medium heat. Stir in the onions, and cook until the onions begin to soften, about 3 minutes. Stir in the flour, and cook 5 minutes longer. Add the milk and bring to a simmer, stirring frequently. Cook and stir until the milk has thickened, about 10 minutes. Once thick and smooth, stir in the salt, white pepper, Worcestershire sauce, hot pepper sauce, mustard, 2 cups of Cheddar cheese, and 1/4 cup of Parmesan cheese. Stir until the cheeses have melted, then stir in the macaroni until evenly coated. Scrape into the prepared baking dish, and smooth the top. Toss the remaining 1 cup Cheddar cheese and 1/4 cup Parmesan cheese with the dry bread crumbs in a mixing bowl. Sprinkle evenly over the top of the macaroni.

4. Bake in the preheated oven until the macaroni is hot and the crust is golden brown, about 30 minutes.

PESTO CHICKEN PENNE CASSEROLE

Servings: 12 - Prep: 15m - Cooks: 1h - Total: 1h15m

NUTRITION FACTS

Calories: 760, Carbohydrates: 40.7g, Fat: 47.2g, Protein: 45.4g, Cholesterol: 114mg

INGREDIENTS

- 1/2 cup seasoned bread crumbs

- 3 cups fresh baby spinach

- 1/2 cup grated Parmesan cheese

- 1 (15 ounce) can crushed tomatoes

- 1 tablespoon olive oil

- 1 (15 ounce) jar Alfredo sauce

- 1 (16 ounce) box penne pasta

- 1 (15 ounce) jar pesto sauce

- 6 cups cubed cooked chicken

- 1 1/2 cups milk

- 4 cups shredded Italian cheese blend

DIRECTIONS

1. Preheat an oven to 350 degrees F (175 degrees C). Grease a 9x13-inch baking dish. Combine the bread crumbs, Parmesan cheese, and olive oil in a small bowl until evenly moistened; set aside.

2. Fill a large pot with lightly salted water and bring to a rolling boil over high heat. Once the water is boiling, stir in the penne, and return to a boil. Cook the pasta uncovered, stirring occasionally, until the pasta has cooked through, but is still firm to the bite, about 11 minutes. Drain well in a colander set in the sink.

3. Meanwhile, combine the chicken in a bowl with the Italian cheese blend, spinach, tomatoes, alfredo sauce, pesto sauce, and milk. Stir in the pasta once done, and scoop into the prepared baking dish. Top with the bread crumb mixture.

4. Bake in the preheated oven until bubbly and golden brown on top, 40 to 45 minutes.

BROCCOLI AND TORTELLINI SALAD

Servings: 12 - Prep: 10m - Cooks: 20m - Total: 30m

NUTRITION FACTS

Calories: 322.4, Carbohydrates: 38.7g, Fat: 0g, Protein: 9g, Cholesterol: 20.3mg

INGREDIENTS

- 6 slices bacon

- 3 heads fresh broccoli, cut into florets

- 20 ounces fresh cheese-filled tortellini

- 1 cup raisins

- 1/2 cup mayonnaise

- 1 cup sunflower seeds

- 1/2 cup white sugar

- 1 red onion, finely chopped

- 2 teaspoons cider vinegar

DIRECTIONS

1. Place bacon in a large, deep skillet. Cook over medium high heat until evenly brown. Drain, crumble and set aside.

2. Bring a large pot of lightly salted water to a boil. Cook tortellini in boiling water for 8 to 10 minutes or until al dente. Drain, and rinse under cold water.

3. In a small bowl, mix together mayonnaise, sugar and vinegar to make the dressing.

4. In a large bowl, combine broccoli, tortellini, bacon, raisins, sunflower seeds and red onion. Pour dressing over salad, and toss.

SPINACaH LASAGNA

Servings: 12 - Prep: 35m - Cooks: 1h - Total: 1h50m - Additional: 15m

NUTRITION FACTS

Calories: 360, Carbohydrates: 41.2g, Fat: 13.5g, Protein: 19g, Cholesterol: 48mg

INGREDIENTS

- 20 lasagna noodles
- 1 teaspoon salt
- 2 tablespoons olive oil
- 1 teaspoon dried oregano
- 1 cup chopped fresh mushrooms
- 1 teaspoon dried basil leaves
- 1 cup chopped onion
- 1/2 teaspoon ground black pepper
- 1 tablespoon minced garlic
- 1 egg
- 2 cups fresh spinach
- 3 cups shredded mozzarella cheese
- 3 cups ricotta cheese
- 3 cups tomato pasta sauce
- 2/3 cup grated Romano cheese
- 1 cup grated Parmesan cheese

DIRECTIONS

1. Preheat oven to 350 degrees F (175 degrees C).

2. Bring a large pot of lightly salted water to a boil. Add lasagna noodles and cook for 8 to 10 minutes or until al dente; drain.

3. In a skillet over medium-high heat, cook mushrooms, onions, and garlic in olive oil until onions are tender. Drain excess liquid and cool. Boil spinach for 5 minutes. Drain, then squeeze out excess liquid. Chop spinach.

4. Combine ricotta cheese, Romano cheese, spinach, salt, oregano, basil, pepper, and egg in a bowl. Add cooled mushroom mixture. Beat with an electric mixer on low speed for 1 minute. Lay 5 lasagna noodles in bottom of a 9x13 inch baking dish. Spread one third of the cheese/spinach mixture over noodles. Sprinkle 1 cup mozzarella cheese and 1/3 cup Parmesan cheese on top. Spread 1 cup pasta sauce over cheese. Repeat layering 2 times.

5. Cover dish with aluminum foil and bake in a preheated oven for 1 hour. Cool 15 minutes before serving.

RICOTTA GNOCCHI

Servings: 5 - Prep: 45m - Cooks: 15m - Total: 1hh

NUTRITION FACTS

Calories: 442, Carbohydrates: 27.1g, Fat: 26g, Protein: 22.4g, Cholesterol: 131mg

INGREDIENTS

- 1 (8 ounce) container ricotta cheese
- 3 tablespoons olive oil
- 2 eggs
- 1 tablespoon minced garlic
- 1/2 cup freshly grated Parmesan cheese
- 1 (15.5 ounce) can diced tomatoes
- 1 teaspoon salt
- 1 dash crushed red pepper flakes (optional)
- 1 teaspoon pepper
- 6 basil leaves, finely shredded
- 1 teaspoon garlic powder
- Salt and pepper to taste
- 1 cup all-purpose flour, or as needed
- 8 ounces fresh mozzarella cheese, cut into small chunks

DIRECTIONS

1. Stir together the ricotta cheese, eggs, Parmesan Cheese, salt, pepper, and garlic powder in a large bowl until evenly combined. Mix in 1 cup of flour. Add additional flour if needed to form a soft dough.

2. Divide the dough into 3 or 4 pieces, and roll into 1/2-inch-thick ropes on a floured surface. Cut each rope into 1-inch pieces, and place on a lightly floured baking sheet. Place in the refrigerator until ready to us

3. Heat olive oil in a saucepan over medium heat. Stir in garlic, and cook until softened and fragrant, about 1 minute. Pour in diced tomatoes and red pepper flakes; bring to a simmer over medium-high heat, and cook for 10 minutes. Stir in shredded basil and season to taste with salt and pepper.

4. While sauce is simmering, bring a large pot of lightly salted water to a boil over high heat. Boil the gnocchi until they float to the surface, 1 to 2 minutes, then drain.

5. To assemble the dish, stir the cubed mozzarella cheese into the sauce and allow the heat of the sauce to soften, but not melt the cheese. Place gnocchi into a serving bowl, and spoon sauce overtop.

AWESOME PASTA SALAD

Servings: 16 - Prep: 30m - Cooks: 10m - Total: 40m

NUTRITION FACTS

Calories: 310, Carbohydrates: 25.9g, Fat: 17.7g, Protein: 12.9g, Cholesterol: 31mg

INGREDIENTS

- 1 (16 ounce) package fusilli (spiral) pasta
- 1 large green bell pepper, cut into 1 inch pieces
- 3 cups cherry tomatoes, halved
- 1 (10 ounce) can black olives, drained
- 1/2 pound provolone cheese, cubed
- 1 (4 ounce) jar pimentos, drained
- 1/2 pound salami, cubed
- 1 (8 ounce) bottle Italian salad dressing
- 1/4 pound sliced pepperoni, cut in half

DIRECTIONS

1. Bring a large pot of lightly salted water to a boil. Add pasta, and cook for 8 to 10 minutes or until al dente. Drain, and rinse with cold water.

2. In a large bowl, combine pasta with tomatoes, cheese, salami, pepperoni, green pepper, olives, and pimentos. Pour in salad dressing, and toss to coat.

RAMEN COLESLAW

Servings: 8 - Prep: 15m - Cooks: 10m - Total: 25m

NUTRITION FACTS

Calories: 253, Carbohydrates: 30.5g, Fat: 12.5g, Protein: 7.1g, Cholesterol: 0mg

INGREDIENTS

- 2 tablespoons vegetable oil
- 1/2 teaspoon ground black pepper
- 3 tablespoons white wine vinegar
- 2 tablespoons sesame seeds
- 2 tablespoons white sugar
- 1/4 cup sliced almonds
- 1 (3 ounce) package chicken flavored ramen noodles, crushed, seasoning packet reserved
- 1/2 medium head cabbage, shredded
- 1/2 teaspoon salt
- 5 green onions, chopped

DIRECTIONS

1. Preheat oven to 350 degrees F (175 degrees C).
2. In a medium bowl, whisk together the oil, vinegar, sugar, ramen noodle spice mix, salt and pepper to create a dressing.
3. Place sesame seeds and almonds in a single layer on a medium baking sheet. Bake in the preheated oven 10 minutes, or until lightly brown.
4. In a large salad bowl, combine the cabbage, green onions and crushed ramen noodles. Pour dressing over the cabbage, and toss to coat evenly. Top with toasted sesame seeds and almonds.

AMAZING ITALIAN LEMON BUTTER CHICKEN

Servings: 6 - Prep: 10m - Cooks: 20m - Total: 30m

NUTRITION FACTS

Calories: 660, Carbohydrates: 37.4g, Fat: 44.9g, Protein: 26.8g, Cholesterol: 155mg

INGREDIENTS

- 1/4 cup white wine
- 1 tablespoon butter
- 5 tablespoons fresh lemon juice
- 1/4 cup all-purpose flour
- 5 tablespoons heavy cream
- salt and pepper to taste

- 1 cup butter, chilled
- 4 ounces bacon
- salt and pepper to taste
- 6 ounces mushrooms, sliced
- 1/2 pound dry farfalle (bow tie) pasta
- 6 ounces artichoke hearts, drained and halved
- 4 skinless, boneless chicken breast halves - pounded to 1/4 inch thickness
- 2 teaspoons capers, drained
- 1 tablespoon olive oil
- chopped fresh parsley for garnish

DIRECTIONS

1. To make the sauce, pour the wine and lemon juice into a saucepan over medium heat. Cook at a low boil until the liquid is reduced by 1/3. Stir in cream, and simmer until it thickens. Gradually add the butter 1 tablespoon at a time to the sauce, stirring until completely incorporated. Season with salt and pepper. Remove from heat, and keep warm.

2. Bring a large pot of lightly salted water to boil. Add pasta, and cook until al dente, about 8 to 10 minutes. Drain, and set aside.

3. To make the chicken, heat oil and 2 tablespoons butter in a large skillet over medium heat. In a bowl, stir together flour, salt, and pepper. Lightly coat chicken with flour mixture. Without crowding, carefully place chicken in hot oil. (If necessary, cook in batches.) Fry until cooked through and golden brown on both sides. Remove the chicken to paper towels. Stir the bacon, mushrooms, artichokes, and capers into the oil; cook until the mushrooms are soft.

4. Cut the chicken breasts into bite-size strips, and return them to the skillet. Stir half of the lemon butter sauce into the chicken mixture.

5. To serve, place pasta in a large bowl. Stir the chicken mixture into the pasta. Taste, and adjust seasonings. Stir in additional lemon butter sauce as desired. Toss well, and garnish with parsley.

MOM'S BEST MACARONI SALAD

Servings: 16 - Prep: 30m - Cooks: 0m - Total: 30m

NUTRITION FACTS

Calories: 424, Carbohydrates: 45g, Fat: 24.7g, Protein: 6.6g, Cholesterol: 19mg

INGREDIENTS

- 16 ounces uncooked elbow macaroni
- 2 cups mayonnaise

- 4 carrots, shredded
- 1 (14 ounce) can sweetened condensed milk
- 1 large red onion, chopped
- 1/2 cup white sugar
- 1/2 green bell pepper, seeded and chopped
- 1/2 cup white vinegar
- 1/2 red bell pepper, seeded and chopped
- salt and pepper to taste
- 1 cup chopped celery

DIRECTIONS

1. Bring a large pot of lightly salted water to a boil. Add macaroni, and cook until tender, about 8 minutes. Rinse under cold water, and drain.

2. In a large bowl, stir together the carrots, red onion, green pepper, red pepper and celery. Mix in the mayonnaise, condensed milk, sugar, vinegar, salt and pepper. Add the macaroni, toss gently, cover and refrigerate for at least 8 hours. I usually make this a day ahead of time, and stir it occasionally to blend the flavors. The macaroni will absorb some of the liquid.

HAMBURGER VEGETABLE SOUP

Servings: 4 - Prep: 5m - Cooks: 25m - Total: 30m

NUTRITION FACTS

Calories: 466, Carbohydrates: 48.9g, Fat: 16.2g, Protein: 33.2g, Cholesterol: 69mg

INGREDIENTS

- 1 pound ground beef
- 2 stalks celery, chopped
- 4 cups chicken broth
- 1 onion, chopped
- 4 cups water
- 1 (16 ounce) package frozen mixed vegetables
- 2 (1 ounce) packages dry onion soup mix
- 3/4 cup elbow macaroni
- 1 (15 ounce) can tomato sauce

DIRECTIONS

1. In a saute pan, brown ground beef, over medium heat.

2. In a large stock pot, combine broth, water, onion soup mix, tomato sauce, celery, onion, frozen vegetables and macaroni. Bring to a boil and then simmer until macaroni is done.

3. Add browned ground beef, mix and serve.

SPINACH AND SUN-DRIED TOMATO PASTA

Servings: 4 - Prep: 15m - Cooks: 25m - Total: 40m

NUTRITION FACTS

Calories: 340, Carbohydrates: 52g, Fat: 8.9g, Protein: 14.7g, Cholesterol: 4mg

INGREDIENTS

- 1 cup vegetable broth
- 1/4 teaspoon crushed red pepper flakes
- 12 dehydrated sun-dried tomatoes
- 1 clove garlic, minced
- 1 (8 ounce) package uncooked penne pasta
- 1 bunch fresh spinach, rinsed and torn into bite-size pieces
- 2 tablespoons pine nuts
- 1/4 cup grated Parmesan cheese
- 1 tablespoon olive oil

DIRECTIONS

1. In a small saucepan, bring the broth to a boil. Remove from heat. Place the sun-dried tomatoes in the broth 15 minutes, or until softened. Drain, reserving broth, and coarsely chop.

2. Bring a large pot of lightly salted water to a boil. Place penne pasta in the pot, cook 9 to 12 minutes, until al dente, and drain.

3. Place the pine nuts in a skillet over medium heat. Cook and stir until lightly toasted.

4. Heat the olive oil and red pepper flakes in a skillet over medium heat, and saute the garlic 1 minute, until tender. Mix in the spinach, and cook until almost wilted. Pour in the reserved broth, and stir in the chopped sun-dried tomatoes. Continue cooking 2 minutes, or until heated through.

5. In a large bowl, toss the cooked pasta with the spinach and tomato mixture and pine nuts. Serve with Parmesan cheese.

SPINACH CHEESE MANICOTTI

Servings: 6 - Prep: 20m - Cooks: 45m - Total: 1h5m

NUTRITION FACTS

Calories: 576, Carbohydrates: 69g, Fat: 20.5g, Protein: 29.8g, Cholesterol: 82mg

INGREDIENTS

- 1 (15 ounce) container ricotta cheese
- 1/4 teaspoon garlic powder
- 1 (10 ounce) package frozen chopped spinach, thawed and squeezed dry
- 1 1/2 cups shredded mozzarella cheese, divided
- 1/2 cup minced onion
- 1/2 cup grated Parmesan cheese, divided
- 1 egg
- 2 (26 ounce) jars spaghetti sauce
- 2 teaspoons minced fresh parsley
- 1 1/2 cups water
- 1/2 teaspoon pepper
- 1 (8 ounce) package manicotti shells

DIRECTIONS

1. Preheat oven to 350 degrees F (175 degrees C).
2. In a large bowl, combine ricotta, spinach, onion and egg. Season with parsley, pepper and garlic powder. Mix in 1 cup mozzarella and 1/4 cup Parmesan. In a separate bowl, stir together spaghetti sauce and water.
3. Spread 1 cup sauce in the bottom of a 9x13 inch baking dish. Stuff uncooked manicotti shells with ricotta mixture, and arrange in a single layer in the dish. Cover with remaining sauce. Sprinkle with remaining mozzarella and Parmesan.
4. Bake in preheated oven for 45 to 55 minutes, or until noodles are soft.

GOULASH SUPREME

Servings: 4 - Prep: 10m - Cooks: 20m - Total: 30m

NUTRITION FACTS

Calories: 565, Carbohydrates: 56.9g, Fat: 25.2g, Protein: 30g, Cholesterol: 85mg

INGREDIENTS

- 1 pound lean ground beef
- 1 tablespoon chili powder
- 1 1/2 cups macaroni
- 1/2 cup chopped onion

- 1 quart stewed tomatoes

- 1 clove garlic, minced

- 2 teaspoons paprika

- 6 ounces tomato paste (optional)

DIRECTIONS

1. In large saucepan brown ground chuck, drain.

2. Add tomatoes, onions, garlic, paprika, chili powder, macaroni and tomato paste, if desired. Add water, a tablespoon at a time, if mixture seems too dry. Simmer until macaroni is tender, about 20 minutes.

CHAMPAGNE SHRIMP AND PASTA

Servings: 4 - Prep: 15m - Cooks: 15m - Total: 30m

NUTRITION FACTS

Calories: 608, Carbohydrates: 38.9g, Fat: 29g, Protein: 31.5g, Cholesterol: 259mg

INGREDIENTS

- 8 ounces angel hair pasta

- 2 tablespoons minced shallots

- 1 tablespoon extra virgin olive oil

- 2 plum tomatoes, diced

- 1 cup sliced fresh mushrooms

- 1 cup heavy cream

- 1 pound medium shrimp, peeled and deveined

- salt and pepper to taste

- 1 1/2 cups champagne

- 3 tablespoons chopped fresh parsley

- 1/4 teaspoon salt

- freshly grated Parmesan cheese

DIRECTIONS

1. Bring a large pot of lightly salted water to a boil. Cook pasta in boiling water for 6 to 8 minutes or until al dente; drain.

2. Meanwhile, heat oil over medium-high heat in a large frying pan. Cook and stir mushrooms in oil until tender. Remove mushrooms from pan, and set aside.

3. Combine shrimp, champagne, and salt in the frying pan, and cook over high heat. When liquid just begins to boil, remove shrimp from pan. Add shallots and tomatoes to champagne; boil until liquid is

reduced to 1/2 cup, about 8 minutes. Stir in 3/4 cup cream; boil until slightly thick, about 1 to 2 minutes. Add shrimp and mushrooms to sauce, and heat through. Adjust seasonings to taste.

4. Toss hot, cooked pasta with remaining 1/4 cup cream and parsley. To serve, spoon shrimp with sauce over pasta, and top with Parmesan cheese.

QUICK AND EASY TUNA CASSEROLE

Servings: 5 - Prep: 5m - Cooks: 25m - Total: 30m

NUTRITION FACTS

Calories: 662, Carbohydrates: 71.8g, Fat: 24.2g, Protein: 38.4g, Cholesterol: 112mg

INGREDIENTS

- 1 (12 ounce) package egg noodles
- 1 onion, chopped
- 2 cups frozen green peas
- 10 slices American processed cheese
- 2 (10.75 ounce) cans condensed cream of mushroom soup
- ground black pepper to taste
- 2 (5 ounce) cans tuna, drained

DIRECTIONS

1. Bring a large pot of water to a boil. Add noodles and frozen peas. Cook until noodles are al dente, drain well. Return noodles and peas to the pot.

2. Mix soup, tuna fish, onions, processed cheese and pepper into the pot. Stir constantly until all of the ingredients are well mixed and the cheese has melted. Serve.

CHEESY ITALIAN TORTELLINI

Servings: 6 - Prep: 15m - Cooks: 8h15m - Total: 8h30m

NUTRITION FACTS

Calories: 468, Carbohydrates: 35.2g, Fat: 24.1g, Protein: 26.9g, Cholesterol: 82mg

INGREDIENTS

- 1/2 pound ground beef
- 1 (14.5 ounce) can Italian-style diced tomatoes, undrained
- 1/2 pound Italian sausage, casings removed
- 1 (9 ounce) package refrigerated or fresh cheese tortellini
- 1 (16 ounce) jar marinara sauce
- 1 cup shredded mozzarella cheese

- 1 (4.5 ounce) can sliced mushrooms
- 1/2 cup shredded Cheddar cheese

DIRECTIONS

1. Crumble the ground beef and Italian sausage into a large skillet. Cook over medium-high heat until browned. Drain.

2. Combine the ground meats, marinara sauce, mushrooms, and tomatoes in a slow cooker. Cover, and cook on LOW heat for 7 to 8 hours.

3. Stir in the tortellini, and sprinkle the mozzarella and cheddar cheese over the top. Cover and cook for 15 more minutes on LOW, or until the tortellini is tender.

GREEK ORZO SALAD

Servings: 6 - Prep: 1h10m - Cooks: 10m - Total: 1h20m

NUTRITION FACTS

Calories: 326, Carbohydrates: 48.7g, Fat: 10.2g, Protein: 13.1g, Cholesterol: 22mg

INGREDIENTS

- 1 1/2 cups uncooked orzo pasta
- 1 (2 ounce) can black olives, drained
- 2 (6 ounce) cans marinated artichoke hearts
- 1/4 cup chopped fresh parsley
- 1 tomato, seeded and chopped
- 1 tablespoon lemon juice
- 1 cucumber, seeded and chopped
- 1/2 teaspoon dried oregano
- 1 red onion, chopped
- 1/2 teaspoon lemon pepper
- 1 cup crumbled feta cheese

DIRECTIONS

1. Bring a large pot of lightly salted water to a boil. Add pasta and cook for 8 to 10 minutes or until al dente; drain. Drain artichoke hearts, reserving liquid.

2. In large bowl combine pasta, artichoke hearts, tomato, cucumber, onion, feta, olives, parsley, lemon juice, oregano and lemon pepper. Toss and chill for 1 hour in refrigerator.

3. Just before serving, drizzle reserved artichoke marinade over salad.

TUNA NOODLE CASSEROLE

Servings: 8 - Prep: 10m - Cooks: 50m - Total: 1h

NUTRITION FACTS

Calories: 467, Carbohydrates: 57.6g, Fat: 16g, Protein: 22.6g, Cholesterol: 30mg

INGREDIENTS

- 1 (16 ounce) package uncooked pasta shells
- 1 teaspoon salt
- 2 (5 ounce) cans tuna, drained
- 1/4 teaspoon ground black pepper
- 1 (10.75 ounce) can condensed cream of mushroom soup
- 1 teaspoon crushed garlic
- 1 (10.75 ounce) can condensed cream of celery soup
- 4 slices processed American cheese
- 1 1/4 cups milk
- 1 1/2 cups crushed potato chips

DIRECTIONS

1. Boil pasta in lightly salted water for 10 minutes, or until al dente; drain well. Return the pasta to the pot it was cooked in.
2. Preheat oven to 350 degrees F (175 degrees C). Spray a 2 1/2 quart casserole dish with cooking spray.
3. Mix tuna with cream of mushroom soup, cream of celery soup, milk, salt, black pepper, and garlic in a medium saucepan. Place pan over medium low heat, and heat through. Alternatively, place these ingredients in a microwave safe dish, and warm in the microwave.
4. Mix tuna mixture with pasta. Spread 1/2 of the noodles into the prepared dish. Arrange the cheese slices over the noodles, then spread the remaining noodle mixture over the cheese. Top with crushed potato chips.
5. Bake, uncovered, for 20 to 30 minutes; cook until the casserole is hot, and the chips begin to brown. Let cool for 10 minutes before serving.

PORTOBELLO MUSHROOM STROGANOFF

Servings: 4 - Prep: 10m - Cooks: 20m - Total: 30m

NUTRITION FACTS

Calories: 525, Carbohydrates: 53.3g, Fat: 30.1g, Protein: 12.8g, Cholesterol: 101mg

INGREDIENTS

- 3 tablespoons butter
- 1 1/2 cups sour cream
- 1 large onion, chopped
- 3 tablespoons all-purpose flour
- 3/4 pound portobello mushrooms, sliced
- 1/4 cup chopped fresh parsley
- 1 1/2 cups vegetable broth
- 8 ounces dried egg noodles

DIRECTIONS

1. Bring a large pot of lightly salted water to a boil. Add egg noodles, and cook until al dente, about 7 minutes. Remove from heat, drain, and set aside.

2. At the same time, melt butter in a large heavy skillet over medium heat. Add onion, and cook, stirring until softened. Turn the heat up to medium-high, and add sliced mushrooms. Cook until the mushrooms are limp and browned. Remove to a bowl, and set aside.

3. In the same skillet, stir in vegetable broth, being sure to stir in any browned bits off the bottom of the pan. Bring to a boil, and cook until the mixture has reduced by 1/3. Reduce heat to low, and return the mushrooms and onion to the skillet.

4. Remove the pan from the heat, stir together the sour cream and flour; then blend into the mushrooms. Return the skillet to the burner, and continue cooking over low heat, just until the sauce thickens. Stir in the parsley, and season to taste with salt and pepper. Serve over cooked egg noodles.

GNOCCHI

Servings: 4 - Prep: 30m - Cooks: 30m - Total: 1h

NUTRITION FACTS

Calories: 329, Carbohydrates: 67g, Fat: 2g, Protein: 9.7g, Cholesterol: 53mg

INGREDIENTS

- 2 potatoes
- 2 cups all-purpose flour
- 1 egg

DIRECTIONS

1. Bring a large pot of salted water to a boil. Peel potatoes and add to pot. Cook until tender but still firm, about 15 minutes. Drain, cool and mash with a fork or potato masher.

2. Combine 1 cup mashed potato, flour and egg in a large bowl. Knead until dough forms a ball. Shape small portions of the dough into long "snakes". On a floured surface, cut snakes into half-inch pieces.

3. Bring a large pot of lightly salted water to a boil. Drop in gnocchi and cook for 3 to 5 minutes or until gnocchi have risen to the top; drain and serve.

NO-CREAM PASTA PRIMAVERA

Servings: 6 - Prep: 25m - Cooks: 35m - Total: 1h

NUTRITION FACTS

Calories: 406, Carbohydrates: 54.4g, Fat: 15.4g, Protein: 13.6g, Cholesterol: 15mg

INGREDIENTS

- 1 (12 ounce) package penne pasta
- 1/4 teaspoon salt
- 1 yellow squash, chopped
- 1/4 teaspoon coarsely ground black pepper
- 1 zucchini, chopped
- 1 tablespoon butter
- 1 carrot, cut into matchsticks
- 1/4 large yellow onion, thinly sliced
- 1/2 red bell peppers, cut into matchsticks
- 2 cloves garlic, thinly sliced
- 1/2 pint grape tomatoes
- 2 teaspoons lemon zest
- 1 cup fresh green beans, trimmed and cut into 1 inch pieces
- 1/3 cup chopped fresh basil leaves
- 5 spears asparagus, trimmed and cut into 1 inch pieces
- 1/3 cup chopped fresh parsley
- 1/4 cup olive oil, divided
- 3 tablespoons balsamic vinegar
- 1 tablespoon Italian seasoning
- 1/2 cup grated Romano cheese
- 1/2 tablespoon lemon juice

DIRECTIONS

1. Preheat oven to 450 degrees F (230 degrees C). Line a baking sheet with aluminum foil.
2. Bring a large pot of lightly salted water to a boil. Add penne pasta and cook until tender yet firm to the bite, 10 to 12 minutes; drain.

3. Toss squash, zucchini, carrot, red bell pepper, tomatoes, green beans, and asparagus together in a bowl with 2 tablespoons olive oil, salt, pepper, lemon juice, and Italian seasoning. Arrange vegetables on the lined baking sheet.

4. Roast vegetables in preheated oven until tender, about 15 minutes.

5. Heat remaining olive oil and butter in a large skillet. Cook onion and garlic in hot oil until tender, 5 to 7 minutes. Mix cooked pasta, lemon zest, basil, parsley, and balsamic vinegar into the onion mixture. Gently toss and cook until heated through, 3 to 5 minutes. Remove from heat and transfer to a large bowl. Toss with roasted vegetables and sprinkle with Romano cheese.

SHRIMP AND ASPARAGUS

Servings: 8 - Prep: 20m - Cooks: 30m - Total: 50m

NUTRITION FACTS

Calories: 653, Carbohydrates: 45.4g, Fat: 42.2g, Protein: 24.7g, Cholesterol: 199mg

INGREDIENTS

- 1 pound fresh asparagus
- 1 tablespoon lemon juice
- 1 (16 ounce) package egg noodles
- 1 pound medium shrimp - peeled and deveined
- 4 cloves garlic, minced
- 1 pound fresh mushrooms, thinly sliced
- 1/2 cup extra virgin olive oil
- 1/2 cup grated Parmesan cheese
- 1 cup butter
- salt and pepper to taste

DIRECTIONS

1. In a small saucepan, boil or steam asparagus in enough water to cover until tender; chop and set aside.

2. Bring a large pot of salted water to full boil, place the pasta in the pot and return to a rolling boil; cook until al dente. Drain well.

3. In a large saucepan, saute garlic in the olive oil over medium-low heat until the garlic is golden brown.

4. Place butter and lemon juice in the saucepan. Heat until the butter has melted. Place the shrimp in the saucepan and cook until the shrimp turns pink. Place the mushrooms and asparagus into the saucepan, cook until mushrooms are tender.

5. Toss the shrimp and vegetable mixture with the egg noodles and sprinkle with Parmesan cheese. Salt and pepper to taste. Serve immediately.

BASIC BAKED SPAGHETTI

Servings: 6 - Prep: 20m - Cooks: 30m - Total: 50m

NUTRITION FACTS

Calories: 546, Carbohydrates: 67.1g, Fat: 17.7g, Protein: 27.7g, Cholesterol: 63mg

INGREDIENTS

- 3/4 pound lean ground beef
- 1 pound spaghetti
- 1 (16 ounce) jar spaghetti sauce
- 1 cup shredded mild Cheddar cheese

DIRECTIONS

1. Preheat oven to 350 degrees F (175 degrees C). In large skillet, cook hamburger until brown. Mix spaghetti sauce into skillet. Reduce heat and simmer.
2. Meanwhile, bring a large pot of lightly salted water to a boil. Mix in pasta and cook for 8 to 10 minutes or until al dente; drain.
3. Mix together spaghetti and meat mixture, pour into 9x13 pan. Top with cheese and bake for 30 minutes, or until heated through and cheese is bubbly.

ITALIAN VEGETABLE SOUP

Servings: 8 - Prep: 20m - Cooks: 50m - Total: 1h10m

NUTRITION FACTS

Calories: 441, Carbohydrates: 52.5g, Fat: 16.6g, Protein: 22.4g, Cholesterol: 48mg

INGREDIENTS

- 1 pound ground beef
- 2 cups water
- 1 cup chopped onion
- 5 teaspoons beef bouillon granules
- 1 cup chopped celery
- 1 tablespoon dried parsley
- 1 cup chopped carrots
- 1/2 teaspoon dried oregano
- 2 cloves garlic, minced
- 1/2 teaspoon dried basil
- 1 (14.5 ounce) can peeled and diced tomatoes

- 2 cups chopped cabbage
- 1 (15 ounce) can tomato sauce
- 1 (15.25 ounce) can whole kernel corn
- 2 (19 ounce) cans kidney beans, drained and rinsed
- 1 (15 ounce) can green beans
- 1 cup macaroni

DIRECTIONS

1. Place ground beef in a large soup pot. Cook over medium heat until evenly browned. Drain excess fat. Stir in onion, celery, carrots, garlic, chopped tomatoes, tomato sauce, beans, water and bouillon. Season with parsley, oregano and basil. Simmer for 20 minutes.

2. Stir in cabbage, corn, green beans and pasta. Bring to a boil, then reduce heat. Simmer until vegetables are tender and pasta is al dente. Add more water if needed.

GROUND BEEF STROGANOFF

Servings: 4 - Prep: 10m - Cooks: 20m - Total: 30m

NUTRITION FACTS

Calories: 696, Carbohydrates: 45.9g, Fat: 44g, Protein: 29.4g, Cholesterol: 139mg

INGREDIENTS

- 1 pound ground beef
- 1/2 cup sour cream
- 1/2 cup chopped onion
- 1/2 cup mayonnaise
- 1 (4.5 ounce) can mushrooms, drained
- 1/2 cup beef broth
- 1/2 teaspoon garlic powder
- 1 (8 ounce) package wide egg noodles
- 1/2 teaspoon mustard powder

DIRECTIONS

1. Break up ground meat into a large skillet, and add onion, mushrooms, garlic powder, and mustard powder. Cook and stir over medium heat until the meat is browned and onion is tender. Drain off excess fat.

2. In a small bowl, combine sour cream, mayonnaise, and beef broth. Stir into beef mixture, and cook over low heat for 10 to 15 minutes. Do not stir too much.

3. Meanwhile, cook pasta in a large pot of boiling water until done. Drain. Serve sauce over hot noodles.

ALYSIA'S BASIC MEAT LASAGNA

Servings: 10 - Prep: 50m - Cooks: 45m - Total: 1h35m

NUTRITION FACTS

Calories: 567, Carbohydrates: 35.6g, Fat: 31.4g, Protein: 36g, Cholesterol: 130mg

INGREDIENTS

- 1 1/2 pounds ground beef
- 1 (8 ounce) package mozzarella cheese, shredded
- 1 teaspoon garlic powder
- 8 ounces provolone cheese, shredded
- 1 (28 ounce) jar sausage flavored spaghetti sauce
- 1 (15 ounce) container ricotta cheese
- 1 (8 ounce) can tomato sauce
- 2 eggs
- 1 teaspoon dried oregano
- 1/4 cup milk
- 1 tablespoon olive oil
- 1/2 teaspoon dried oregano
- 4 cloves garlic, minced
- 9 lasagna noodles
- 1 small onion, diced
- 1/4 cup grated Parmesan cheese

DIRECTIONS

1. Preheat oven to 375 degrees F (190 degrees C).
2. Season ground beef with garlic powder. Heat a large skillet over medium-high heat. Cook and stir ground beef in the hot skillet until browned and crumbly, 5 to 7 minutes. Drain and discard grease.
3. Pour spaghetti sauce, tomato sauce, and oregano into a large saucepan. Set aside.
4. Heat olive oil in a large skillet over medium-high heat. Saute garlic and onions until softened and translucent, about 5 minutes. Place cooked onion-garlic mixture and cooked ground beef into the sauce mixture. Cover and let simmer for 15 to 20 minutes.
5. Combine mozzarella and provolone cheeses in a medium bowl. Mix ricotta cheese, eggs, milk, and 1/2 teaspoon oregano together in a separate bowl.
6. Layer a 9x13-inch baking pan with just enough sauce to cover the bottom of the pan. Lay three lasagna noodles in the pan over the sauce. Cover with more sauce, then with ricotta mixture then sprinkle with

mozzarella/provolone mixture; repeat layering. Finish with a layer of noodles and remaining sauce. Sprinkle top with Parmesan cheese.

7. Bake, covered, in the preheated oven for 30 minutes. Uncover and continue to bake until cheese is melted and top is golden, about 15 minutes more.

GREEK PASTA WITH TOMATOES AND WHITE BEANS

Servings: 4 - Prep: 10m - Cooks: 15m - Total: 25m

NUTRITION FACTS

Calories: 460, Carbohydrates: 79g, Fat: 5.9g, Protein: 23.4g, Cholesterol: 17mg

INGREDIENTS

- 2 (14.5 ounce) cans Italian-style diced tomatoes
- 8 ounces penne pasta
- 1 (19 ounce) can cannellini beans, drained and rinsed
- 1/2 cup crumbled feta cheese
- 10 ounces fresh spinach, washed and chopped

DIRECTIONS

1. Cook the pasta in a large pot of boiling salted water until al dente.
2. Meanwhile, combine tomatoes and beans in a large non-stick skillet. Bring to a boil over medium high heat. Reduce heat, and simmer 10 minutes.
3. Add spinach to the sauce; cook for 2 minutes or until spinach wilts, stirring constantly.
4. Serve sauce over pasta, and sprinkle with feta.

ITALIAN SAUSAGE TORTELLINI SOUP

Servings: 6 - Prep: 15m - Cooks: 55m - Total: 1h10m

NUTRITION FACTS

Calories: 249, Carbohydrates: 27.7g, Fat: 8.9g, Protein: 12.4g, Cholesterol: 22g

INGREDIENTS

- 1 (3.5 ounce) link sweet Italian sausage, casings removed
- 1/2 teaspoon dried basil
- 1 cup chopped onions
- 1/2 teaspoon dried oregano
- 2 cloves garlic, minced

- 1 cup tomato sauce
- 5 cups beef stock
- 1 zucchini, chopped
- 1/3 cup water
- 8 ounces cheese tortellini
- 1/2 cup red wine
- 1 green bell pepper, chopped
- 4 tomatoes - peeled, seeded and chopped
- 1 tablespoon chopped fresh parsley
- 1 cup chopped carrots
- 2 tablespoons grated Parmesan cheese for topping

DIRECTIONS

1. Place the sausage in a large pot over medium high heat and saute for 10 minutes, or until well browned. Drain the fat except for about 1 tablespoon, add the onions and garlic and saute for 5 more minutes.
2. Next add the beef stock, water, wine, tomatoes, carrots, basil, oregano and tomato sauce. Bring to a boil, reduce heat to low and simmer for 30 minutes, skimming any fat that may surface.
3. Add the zucchini, tortellini, green bell pepper and parsley to taste. Simmer for 10 minutes, or until tortellini is fully cooked. Pour into individual bowls and garnish with the cheese.

EASY LASAGNA

Servings: 8 - Prep: 35m - Cooks: 1h - Total: 1h45m - Additional: 10m

NUTRITION FACTS

Calories: 702, Carbohydrates: 62.5g, Fat: 30.3g, Protein: 44.2g, Cholesterol: 142mg

INGREDIENTS

- 1 pound lean ground beef
- 1 pint part-skim ricotta cheese
- 1 onion, chopped
- 1/4 cup grated Parmesan cheese
- 1 (4.5 ounce) can mushrooms, drained
- 2 eggs
- 1 (28 ounce) jar spaghetti sauce
- 1 (16 ounce) package lasagna noodles
- 1 (16 ounce) package cottage cheese
- 8 ounces shredded mozzarella cheese

DIRECTIONS

1. Preheat oven to 350 degrees F (175 degrees C).

2. In a large skillet, cook and stir ground beef until brown. Add mushrooms and onions; saute until onions are transparent. Stir in pasta sauce, and heat through.

3. In a medium size bowl, combine cottage cheese, ricotta cheese, grated Parmesan cheese, and eggs.

4. Spread a thin layer of the meat sauce in the bottom of a 13x9 inch pan. Layer with uncooked lasagna noodles, cheese mixture, mozzarella cheese, and meat sauce. Continue layering until all ingredients are used, reserving 1/2 cup mozzarella. Cover pan with aluminum foil.

5. Bake in preheated oven for 45 minutes. Uncover, and top with remaining half cup of mozzarella cheese. Bake for an additional 15 minutes. Remove from oven, and let stand 10 to 15 minutes before serving.

INCREDIBLY EASY CHICKEN AND NOODLES

Servings: 6 - Prep: 10m - Cooks: 30m - Total: 40m

NUTRITION FACTS

Calories: 504, Carbohydrates: 54.8g, Fat: 19.6g, Protein: 27.4g, Cholesterol: 99mg

INGREDIENTS

- 1 (26 ounce) can condensed cream of chicken soup
- 2 teaspoons onion powder
- 1 (10.75 ounce) can condensed cream of mushroom soup
- 1 teaspoon seasoning salt
- 3 (14.5 ounce) cans chicken broth
- 1/2 teaspoon garlic powder
- 2 cups diced, cooked chicken breast meat
- 2 (9 ounce) packages frozen egg noodles

DIRECTIONS

1. In a large pot, mix the cream of chicken soup, cream of mushroom soup, chicken broth, and chicken meat. Season with onion powder, seasoning salt, and garlic powder. Bring to a boil, and stir in the noodles. Reduce heat to low, and simmer for 20 to 30 minutes.

GROUND TURKEY CASSEROLE

Servings: 8 - Prep: 30m - Cooks: 35m - Total: 1h5m

NUTRITION FACTS

Calories: 516, Carbohydrates: 31.8g, Fat: 31.5g, Protein: 26.9g, Cholesterol: 145mg

INGREDIENTS

- 1 pound ground turkey
- 1 (8 ounce) package cream cheese
- 1 (15 ounce) can tomato sauce
- 1 (12 ounce) package uncooked egg noodles
- 1 teaspoon white sugar
- 2 cups shredded Cheddar cheese
- 1 (8 ounce) container sour cream

DIRECTIONS

1. Preheat oven to 350 degrees F (175 degrees C).

2. In a large skillet over medium-high heat, saute the ground turkey for 5 to 10 minutes, or until browned. Drain the turkey, stir in the tomato sauce and sugar, and set aside. In a medium bowl, combine the sour cream and cream cheese. Mix well and set aside.

3. Cook noodles according to package directions. Place them into a 9x13-inch baking dish, then layer the turkey mixture over the noodles. Then layer the sour cream mixture over the turkey, and top with cheese.

4. Bake at 350 degrees F (175 degrees C) for 20 to 35 minutes, or until cheese is melted and bubbly.

PEANUT NOODLES

Servings: 3 - Prep: 10m - Cooks: 15m - Total: 25m

NUTRITION FACTS

Calories: 568, Carbohydrates: 70.1g, Fat: 24.8g, Protein: 19.7g, Cholesterol: 0mg

INGREDIENTS

- 8 ounces spaghetti
- 1/4 cup soy sauce
- 1 bunch green onions, sliced (white parts only)
- 1/4 cup hot water
- 2 tablespoons sesame oil
- 1 tablespoon cider vinegar
- 1 teaspoon minced fresh ginger root
- 1 teaspoon white sugar
- 1/3 cup peanut butter
- 1/4 teaspoon crushed red pepper flakes

DIRECTIONS

1. Cook pasta in a large pot of boiling water until done. Drain.

2. Meanwhile, combine oil and onions in a small skillet. Saute over low heat until tender. Add ginger; cook and stir for 1 to 2 minutes. Mix in peanut butter, soy sauce, water, vinegar, sugar, and red pepper flakes. Remove from heat.

3. Toss noodles with sauce, and serve.

ANGEL HAIR PASTA WITH GARLIC SHRIMP AND BROCCOLI

Servings: 6 - Prep: 30m - Cooks: 30m - Total: 1h

NUTRITION FACTS

Calories: 430.7, Carbohydrates: 39.5g, Fat: 0g, Protein: 24.3g, Cholesterol: 144.8mg

INGREDIENTS

- 1 (12 ounce) package angel hair pasta
- 2 tablespoons grated Parmesan cheese
- 2 1/2 tablespoons butter, divided
- 2 teaspoons salt, divided
- 1 1/2 tablespoons all-purpose flour
- 1/2 teaspoon ground white pepper
- 1 1/2 cups milk
- 1 dash Worcestershire sauce
- 1/2 cup heavy cream
- 1 dash hot sauce
- 1 1/2 tablespoons pesto
- 1/2 (16 ounce) package frozen broccoli florets, thawed
- 1 1/2 tablespoons chopped fresh parsley
- 1 pound jumbo shrimp, peeled and deveined
- 3 cloves garlic, minced
- 3 cloves garlic, minced

DIRECTIONS

1. Bring a large pot of lightly salted water to a boil. Add pasta and cook for 8 to 10 minutes or until al dente; drain.

2. Melt 1.5 tablespoons butter in a medium saucepan over medium heat. Stir in flour and cook for 2 minutes. Slowly stir in milk and cream; simmer, stirring constantly, until thickened. Mix in pesto, parsley, 3 cloves minced garlic, Parmesan cheese, 1 teaspoon salt, white pepper, Worcestershire sauce and hot sauce. Reduce heat to low and allow to simmer.

3. Meanwhile, place broccoli in a steamer over 1 inch of boiling water, and cover. Cook until tender but still firm, about 2 to 6 minutes. Drain.

4. Melt 1 tablespoon butter in a large skillet. Saute shrimp, remaining 3 cloves minced garlic, and 1 teaspoon salt for 5 minutes, or until shrimp are pink.

5. In a large bowl, toss pasta, shrimp and broccoli; pour sauce over and serve.

HAM TETRAZZINI

Servings: 4 - Prep: 15m - Cooks: 15m - Total: 30m

NUTRITION FACTS

Calories: 358, Carbohydrates: 38.8g, Fat: 15.6g, Protein: 15.1g, Cholesterol: 39mg

INGREDIENTS

- 6 ounces spaghetti
- 1/2 cup water
- 3 quarts water
- 1/2 cup shredded Cheddar cheese
- 1 teaspoon salt
- 1 cup diced ham
- 1 tablespoon butter
- 2 tablespoons chopped fresh parsley
- 2 tablespoons chopped onion
- 2 tablespoons chopped pimento peppers
- 1 (10.75 ounce) can condensed cream of mushroom soup

DIRECTIONS

1. Bring a large pot of lightly salted water to a boil. Add spaghetti and cook for 8 to 10 minutes or until al dente; drain (or use leftover pasta; see Cook's Note).

2. While pasta is cooking, melt butter in a saucepan over medium heat. Stir in onion; cook and stir until the onion has softened and turned translucent, about 5 minutes.

3. Stir in cream of mushroom soup, 1/2 cup water, and shredded cheese. Heat mixture until cheese melts, stirring often.

4. Mix in the ham, cooked and drained pasta, chopped pimento, and chopped parsley to saucepan; stir to combine. Cook until mixture is heated through, then serve.

SHRIMP AND FETA CHEESE PASTA

Servings: 5 - Prep: 15m - Cooks: 15m - Total: 30m

NUTRITION FACTS

Calories: 603, Carbohydrates: 75.2g, Fat: 19.5g, Protein: 32.9g, Cholesterol: 168mg

INGREDIENTS

- 3 tablespoons olive oil
- 2 tomatoes, chopped
- 1 pound shrimp, peeled and deveined
- 1 teaspoon dried oregano
- 5 cloves garlic, minced
- 1/2 teaspoon dried basil
- 1 tablespoon white wine
- 1 (6 ounce) package crumbled feta cheese
- 1 pound linguine pasta

DIRECTIONS

1. In a medium skillet over medium heat, heat 2 tablespoons olive oil. Cook shrimp, garlic and white wine for 5 minutes, or until shrimp is pink. Remove shrimp with slotted spoon and set aside.

2. Bring a large pot of lightly salted water to a boil. Add pasta and cook for 8 to 10 minutes or until al dente; drain.

3. While pasta is cooking, cook tomatoes with remaining 1 tablespoon oil, oregano and basil over medium heat in wine mixture until tender, 10 minutes.

4. Toss hot pasta with shrimp, tomato sauce and feta. Feta will melt slightly. Serve.